The Book
of Learning
and Forgetting

BOOKS BY FRANK SMITH

Understanding Reading (five editions)
Writing and the Writer (two editions)
Comprehension and Learning
Reading Without Nonsense* (three editions; Reading in UK)
Insult to Intelligence
to think*
Whose Language? What Power?*
The Book of Learning and Forgetting*

Edited Volumes
The Genesis of Language (with George A. Miller)
Psycholinguistics and Reading
Awakening to Literacy (with Hillel Goelman and
    Antoinette A. Oberg)

Essays
Essays Into Literacy
Joining the Literacy Club
Between Hope and Havoc

* Published by Teachers College Press

The Book
of Learning
and Forgetting

FRANK SMITH

TEACHERS
COLLEGE
PRESS

Teachers College, Columbia University
New York and London

Published by Teachers College Press, 1234 Amsterdam Ave., New York, NY 10027

Cover illustration: Detail from *Die Malkunst* (The Artist in His Studio) by Johannes van Delft Vermeer (1632–1675), reproduced by permission of the Kunsthistorisches Museum, Vienna.

Library of Congress Cataloging-in-Publication Data

Smith, Frank, 1928–
    The boook of learning and forgetting / Frank Smith.
       p.   cm.
    Includes bibliographic references (p.   ) and index.
    ISBN 0-8077-3750-X (paper : alk. paper)
    1. Learning, Psychology of.   2. Memory.   I. Title.
  LB1060.S55   1998
  370.15'23—dc21   98-5374

ISBN 0-8077-3750-X   (paper)

Printed on acid-free paper

Manufactured in the United States of America

10 09 08 07 06   7   8   9   10   11

Contents

Preface

The fact that making an effort is an inefficient way to learn—and an almost certain way to forget—comes as a surprise to many people. They have been taught that learning demands hard work, serious motivation, and focused concentration. They may even have been taught that they shouldn't expect very much success in learning, no matter how hard they try.

In this book I contrast two visions of learning: an "official" theory that learning is work and a "classic" view that we learn effortlessly every moment of our waking lives. We all share and respect the classic view, which is embedded deep beneath our consciousness, though we are rarely aware that we do so. I look extensively at the rich, complex, and long-lasting learning that we accomplish from birth, unconsciously and inconspicuously, and I examine in detail the origins and history of the contrary belief and the way in which it has come to dominate educational systems.

On the way I explore many aspects of our mental lives—the way in which we all, as babies, children, and adults, make sense of the world, learn, think, and acquire and express our unique individual identities. I also recount some of the damage and injustices caused at all levels of education, not only by the official view that learning requires work—so that failure to learn can be attributed to laziness—but by the intrusive mass of unnecessary external controls in which teaching and learning have become embedded, including testing, grading, and contrived competitiveness.

The widespread propagation of the official theory is not so much a conspiracy as a massive manifestation of self-interest by special-interest groups outside schools. The belief has been fostered by academic psychology, uncritically adopted in education, and vigorously promoted by people who would like to control what students and teachers do in schools—often to make a profit in the bargain. The idea has been around long enough—just more than 100 years—to have become widely accepted as common sense, natural, the way things have to be. And the official theory is wrong. It creates frustration and wasted effort in our personal lives and futility and discrimination in schools. It is a crippling belief that fosters some of the worst social attitudes that afflict our society.

I begin this book by reviewing the manner in which we all learn continuously and without noticeable effort. This is a celebration of the power of the human brain—even though there is a constant danger that we may learn something that is not in our best interest. The history of how the official theory of learning developed and gained its paralyzing hold is a miserable topic, and I leave it to the second part of the book.

Finally, I discuss how we can all protect ourselves and our children from the most destructive effects of the official theory of learning—and how, eventually, after a century of domination, the sterile theory might itself be put to rout, bringing an end to all the personal and social damage it has produced.

As a cognitive psychologist, I have studied and researched the human brain, particularly with respect to language, learning, and understanding, for more than 25 years. During this time I have had the privilege of working in hundreds of schools around the world, with many thousands of teachers and students. This book summarizes my findings.

These findings present a choice to teachers and everyone else concerned with education (including their own education). One option is to continue in subservience to an artificial theory of learning, with its inevitable inefficiency, forgetting, frustration, and victimization of both teachers and students. The other option is to acknowledge and work with the natural strengths of the human brain.

The best time to start working with those natural strengths might be now. Please don't read this book determined to remember everything of significance you think you might find in it. If you do, you'll probably forget what you read very quickly, most of it before you reach the end of the book. And you'll find the book more difficult to understand as well.

But if you relax and simply read the book for interest you'll probably enjoy it more, learn more than you expect, and be less likely to forget points that are most relevant to you.

I
WHAT'S GOING ON HERE?

Consider a student—a child in the primary grades or a mature adult in graduate school. After weeks of hard study the student has taken a test that could play a large part in his or her career. The instructor solemnly reports the score. "C-minus again," the instructor observes. "You haven't learned very much, have you?"

But the student has, on the contrary, learned a great deal. The student has registered the condemnatory look on the instructor's face, experienced the sickening feeling in the stomach, and concluded once more what a fruitless and punishing experience the entire learning situation can be. The student has lost a bit more confidence—and is unlikely to forget any of it.

When we talk about learning in such a situation, can we be talking about two different things? And if we are, why do we give the two things the same name? Is something crucial going on that isn't paid attention to in school?

When some people complain that students don't learn very much in school and blame lack of ability or effort on the part of the students or their teachers, what kind of learning are they talking about? Why do they focus so much on what students fail to learn, rather than on what they are learning in its place, which may have much more significance in the students' lives?

What's going on here? How can we forget so rapidly what we try so hard to learn—and learn so effortlessly what we might often prefer to forget? The explanation lies in the tale of two visions.

1

A Tale of
Two Visions

Th*his* is a tale of two visions, of two conflicting points of view, about matters central to everyone's life: learning and forgetting.

I refer to one vision as *the classic view of learning and forgetting*. It is classic because it is archetypal, universal, deeply rooted, and uncontaminated. It says, very simply, that we learn from people around us with whom we identify. We can't help learning from them, and we learn without knowing that we are learning.

We all recognize implicitly the influence that other people have on ourselves and on our children, and the fact that it is almost impossible to forget what is learned in this way. We act on this belief throughout our lives, especially as far as our children are concerned. We know the likelihood of their becoming like the people with whom they associate and identify most.

But it is only comparatively recently that extensive research has documented the huge amounts of permanent learning that everyone achieves, inconspicuously and effortlessly, in the manner outlined by the classic point of view. Just about all the important knowledge we have about our personal worlds, and the skills we have developed to navigate through these worlds, are a direct result of learning in the classic way.

It is not only things that are useful to know that we learn in this way. We also, unfortunately, learn things that we might be better off not learning, such as the fact that there are certain things we shouldn't expect to be able to learn, or that we have certain (usually fictitious) learning deficiencies or disabilities. We can learn that we are "not the kind of person" who is expected to learn certain things, which can handicap us throughout our lives and create enormous difficulties in education.

There is an alternative to the classic view that is preeminent, coercive, manipulative, discriminatory—and wrong. It is a theory that learning is work, and that anything can be learned provided sufficient effort is expended and sufficient control enforced. The theory has gained supreme power in educational systems from kindergarten to university. It has become so pervasive that many people can't imagine an alternative to it.

This is the view—I call it *the official theory of learning and forgetting*—that is responsible for

- compelling people to try to learn in the most inefficient way possible, with rapid forgetting guaranteed,
- persuading individuals that they won't learn unless they make a determined effort, and that the fault is theirs if they fail,
- segregating learners at school so they can't help each other, in the process making life as difficult as possible for teachers,
- coercing learners and teachers into ineffective programs of study, designed by distant authorities who have no way of knowing or rectifying the difficulties they create,
- forcing learners and teachers to waste their time on repetitive exercises and drills that teach only that learning is frustrating and difficult,
- imposing discriminatory and discouraging "tests" that ensure that individuals who most need help and encouragement get the least,
- convincing teachers, learners, and parents that the most important thing about education is scores and grades,
- making learning a trial when it should be a pleasure, and making forgetting inevitable when it should be insignificant.

There is more, but that is enough for now. The official theory that learning is simply a question of effort is so endemic that it is widely regarded as unchallengeable, natural, and time-honored, a matter of "getting back to basics." But the official view is none of these; it is relatively recent and totally artificial, a theory contrived solely for purposes of control, first in experimental laboratories, then in classrooms.

Proponents of the official theory dismiss the classic view—if they acknowledge it at all—as "unscientific," "folk psychology," or "unsubstantiated." They may even call it faddish. But unlike the official theory, the classic view is supported by thousands of years of experience in every culture in the world.[1]

The following chart indicates the ways in which the two visions differ. These differences need not be memorized—they summarize characteristics of each vision that will become apparent in the chapters that follow.

The classic view says that learning is	*The official theory says that learning is*
continual	occasional
effortless	hard work
inconspicuous	obvious
boundless	limited
unpremeditated	intentional
independent of rewards and punishment	dependent on rewards and punishment
based on self-image	based on effort
vicarious	individualistic
never forgotten	easily forgotten
inhibited by testing	assured by testing
a social activity	an intellectual activity
growth	memorization

Because it is so obvious that people often have to struggle to learn what we would like them to learn, and what they would like to learn for themselves, I emphasize now what I reiterate throughout the book. Learning is not hard work. Something is being learned, whether we want it or not, all the time. But achieving the necessary circumstances and frame of mind for desired learning may be very difficult indeed. Desired learning, and the overcoming or avoidance of detrimental learning, may sometimes demand special conditions and exceptional patience and talent. For all that to take place, we must understand learning and forgetting.

The official theory should be forgotten—but it can't be. Ironically, we didn't learn the official theory intentionally, the way the official theory claims that all learning must take place. If that had been the case, we might forget it easily. Instead, we learned the official theory in precisely the lasting but inconspicuous manner that the classic point of view explains, from the attitudes and behavior of people around us.

The official theory became an unquestioned part of most of us because it permeates the broad educational culture in which we have grown up. It is usually taken for granted, and it will not be eradicated from our minds. Instead we must learn—in the classic manner—that the official theory is unsound and dangerous, and we must help each other to gain confidence in the alternative point of view, which all the real-world evidence (as opposed to that from psychological laboratories) demonstrates is right.

II

THE CLASSIC VIEW OF LEARNING AND FORGETTING

2

A Question of Identity

The classic view of learning is encapsulated in seven words familiar to every speaker of English: *You learn from the company you keep.* You don't learn by consciously modeling yourself on the company you keep, or by deliberately imitating other people. You *become* like them. We all know this and organize our lives accordingly. I have found a similar proverb or saying in every language I have encountered.

We take it for granted that the people around us influence the way we are. That is why the point of view is classic—we rarely think about the continual learning that we and others do all the time. And this is learning that is *permanent*. We rarely forget the interests, attitudes, beliefs, and skills that we acquire simply by interacting with the significant people in our lives.

LEARNING WITHOUT AWARENESS

There is no way to catalog all the knowledge and skills an individual learns in the course of a lifetime. That would require unraveling an entire mind, and would reveal a content too vast and intricate even to attempt to itemize. Think of the complexity of our own daily lives, the objects and events that we encounter in our neighborhoods, in our travels, or through the media. Our brains must be at least as complicated as the world through which we move. Yet how much of this knowledge was acquired in the classroom or through any kind of deliberate study?

There are two ways to illustrate everyone's continual and effort-less learning. The first is to give a few simple examples, and the second is to make a detailed examination of just one or two aspects of all the learning we accomplish throughout our lives, without being aware of it. I shall do both.

Consider first the concern parents often have about the company their children keep. We know the enormous influence that friends have. If our children have friends who play hockey, we are not surprised when we begin to get requests for hockey equipment and for tickets to hockey games. If their friends hang out in small groups around parking lots, we might begin to get anxious. We visit the schools our son or daughter might attend, not so much to see the school facilities or the teachers' lesson plans as to observe the other students. We know that if our children attend a particular school they will finish up looking, talking, and behaving like the other students. I have never heard a parent say, "I'm not worried about the gang my son goes with—he's a slow learner." Parents know that children learn from their friends, particularly the things the parents would prefer their children not learn. And they also know that what their children learn in this way will be very difficult to erase. It is life-long learning.

It is a frightening thought for many teachers that their students are learning all the time. Without any forgetting. And the students can't help it. They can even learn things they might be better off not learn-ing. The problem in school is not that many students aren't learning, but *what* they are learning. They may not learn what their teachers teach them, but their teachers may not be teaching what they think they are teaching. To find out what students actually learn, look at the way they leave school. If they leave thinking that "school things"—such as read-ing, writing, mathematics, or history—are boring, difficult, and irrele-vant to their lives and that they are "dummies," this is something they have learned both in school and outside. They *learn* to be nonreaders, or that they are nonspellers, or that they can't do mathematics. They learn who they are. If they learn they are leaders or geniuses (or clowns or fools) they behave accordingly.

Now consider the massive amounts of often unsuspected learning we accomplish throughout our lives from the moment of our birth. I must begin by being a little more specific about what I mean when I reiterate that we learn from the company we keep.

I'm not claiming that we learn from all the people around us. That obviously isn't the case. All sorts of things can go on around us, espe-cially in school situations, and we don't seem to learn a thing, even when other people are most anxious that we should learn. Instead I mean that we learn from the individuals or groups with whom we *identify*.[1]

THE ADVANTAGES OF JOINING CLUBS

I refer to communities of influential people as *clubs*. These may sometimes be the formal organizations that we join and maintain membership in by paying a fee—the political clubs, sports clubs, and social clubs with which we might be affiliated. But clubs may often be the informal associations that we belong to just by sharing an interest and a sense of community—the metaphorical clubs of teachers, parents, students, book readers, gardeners, joggers, or cyclists—all of the different groups with which we identify ourselves.

The way we identify ourselves is at the core of it all. We don't join a club, or stay in it, if we can't identify with the other members. We are uncomfortable if we feel the other members are not the kind of people we see ourselves as being. In fact we'll go out of our way to demonstrate that we are not members of clubs with which we don't want to be identified. We'll do this if we decide that the club doesn't meet our desires or expectations, but we'll also do this if we feel that other members of the club don't want to be associated with us. If we don't feel "one of them," we show that we never wanted to be "one of them."

And as we identify with other members of the clubs to which we belong, so we establish and build up our own identity. Every time we engage in a club activity the other members in effect reaffirm, "You're just like us." And at the same time, we confirm to them, "I'm just like you." (If we reject a club, or are excluded from it, we are told, "You're not one of us." And we respond emphatically, "I'm not like you—and I wouldn't want to be.")

This is the way our identity is established. We don't find out "who we are" by gazing into a mirror and asking profound existential questions. We know who we are—and other people know who we are—from the clubs, formal and informal, with which we associate ourselves; from the company we keep. We begin to worry about our identity if we feel we don't have any link with people around us, especially if we think they may be excluding us. "Who am I?" is inevitably "Who do other people think I am?" whether we realize it or not.

And as we identify with other members of all the clubs to which we belong, so we learn to be like those other members. We become like the company we keep, exhibiting this identity in the way we talk, dress, and ornament ourselves, and in many other ways. The identification creates the possibility of learning. All learning pivots on who we think we are, and who we see ourselves as capable of becoming.[2]

A remarkable characteristic of the learning we do from the company we keep, effortlessly and inconspicuously, is that it is *vicarious*. We

don't have to do anything ourselves in order to learn except put ourselves in the company of people with whom we identify. Other people do
things, and we learn. We don't learn as a consequence of what other
people do; we learn at the moment they do things—always provided
that we see ourselves as members of the club. It is trial and error learning, if you like, but since the trial is performed by the experienced person who will be learned from, not by the inexperienced learner, there is
rarely error. I shall give many examples of the largely error-free way in
which babies learn to talk, to understand speech, and to learn about
the ways of the world in general.

Another notable characteristic of this continual and vicarious learning is that it is *permanent,* or almost so. We usually don't start forgetting the things we learn from the company we keep throughout our
lives, such as the way we talk and the way we feel about ourselves,
until there is massive physical damage or degeneration. We'd often be
much better off if we *could* forget a particular habit we've acquired or
an attitude we may have learned toward ourselves, but the more we try
to forget such things the more we tend to remember them.

We know about the consequences of associating with other people
without ever really thinking about them because what we learn is so
much a part of our lives. We feel it is "natural" to become the kind of
person we are from the company we keep without necessarily regard-
ing the process as learning. If we do think about learning, we are likely to employ the official theory, expecting that learning will be difficult
and effortful. We think—if we think about it at all—that the tremen-
dous amounts of learning we do all our lives, such as learning to talk,
learning and remembering the sports scores that we are interested in,
and remembering where we live and who we are and where we were
last New Year's Eve, as just "memory." We don't call it learning, though
it is. It is, however, quite different from the type of learning with which
the official theory of learning is concerned.

The official theory, which regards learning as work and forgetting
as inevitable, is primarily concerned with *memorization,* the effort to store
away one thing after another. The classic kind of learning, on the other
hand, is *growth.* It is growth of the mind analogous in every way to the
growth of the body.

Physical growth doesn't normally occur sporadically, as the result
of determined effort, nor by the incorporation of a multitude of small
new parts. A two-year-old infant is not two one-year-olds, one on top of
the other. Nor does the two-year-old have more or different parts. A
two-year-old is the same as a one-year-old, except for gains in power, complexity, and maturity. The child has *grown,* as a consequence of appro-

priate nourishment and exercise. And if at any time the child isn't appropriately nourished and exercised, then the child's physical development will be stunted and distorted.

It's the same with mental growth. We learn "new things" from the company we keep by making them part of what we already know. They are not new bits to be added to a store of knowledge, but extensions or elaborations of the experience and beliefs that make us what we are. And if at any time our minds aren't appropriately nourished and exercised, then our mental development will be stunted and distorted.

Useful learning doesn't occur when we take time out of our normal lives and knuckle down to serious study. Learning is an inevitable part of our normal lives, and it only takes place, in any useful way, when we are in a normal frame of mind. The main thing we learn when we struggle to learn is that learning is a struggle.

3

The Immensity of Children's Learning

Do you know the number of words children have learned by the time they get to school at the age of five or six? If all parents and teachers were familiar with this figure they might have some understanding of how much learning children are capable of accomplishing without formal instruction, tests, and all of the other rigmarole that goes along with our educational systems. The answer is that by the age of six children have a vocabulary of about 10,000 words.

They don't all know the same 10,000 words, of course. They know 10,000 words that their friends know. They don't know all the words their teachers know—but they probably know some words their teachers don't know. Since birth, children have been learning new words at the rate of 2000 per year, without conspicuous effort or organized instruction—and without any forgetting. Psychologist George Miller calculated that infants are learning (and remembering) one new word for every hour they are awake. If that is true, the children he studied couldn't have been sleeping very much.[1]

Why are most teachers unaware of all this inconspicuous learning, given that one of their primary concerns should be how much their students know? Part of the answer is that education professors—the teachers of teachers—usually focus on what they think teachers and students *can't do*. They emphasize the central role they believe must be played by outside experts (including themselves, of course).

WORDS AREN'T EVERYTHING

I'm going to say a great deal about words, because that is one of the
most conspicuous parts of anyone's language. It's not difficult to notice
the relative richness or poverty of someone's vocabulary, and it is not
much more difficult to estimate the size of it, though that is rarely done.

I shall also make some reference to grammar because that is another conspicuous aspect of language by which children, and adults as well,
are frequently judged and compared.

But I don't want to suggest that language consists of just vocabulary and grammar, or even that they constitute the largest and most important part of our language learning. There is much about spoken language
that is rarely talked about, such as phrasing, intonation, taking turns in
conversation, and just how loud and long it is appropriate to say something, for the simple reason that it is *too complicated* to talk about. We
don't know enough about these aspects of language to try to teach them
so we tend to ignore them or to dismiss them as insignificant. The situation is the same in writing, where we concentrate on matters such as spelling
and punctuation because they are conspicuous, but we give up on such vital
but complicated matters as paragraphing, style, and the appropriate way
in which to write different kinds of text for different audiences and different purposes, which all writers need to know about.

But the fact that there is much we aren't explicitly taught doesn't
mean that we haven't been learning. We learn without knowing that
we are learning. We learn without knowing *what* we are learning. In fact,
there are many things we know that we don't know we have learned,
though they dominate much of our behavior and our interactions with
other people.

Take for example the matter of eye contact—how long you can look
into someone's eyes and hold their gaze. This is an important issue for
personal relationships. Two people gazing into each other's eyes are demonstrating intimacy. One person doing this while the other looks elsewhere is demonstrating authority. One person avoiding another's gaze
is demonstrating embarrassment or wariness, if not shiftiness. The rules
are incredibly precise—a couple of milliseconds makes a difference. But
they are also incredibly complex—it makes a difference what you are
talking about, with whom you are talking, and the circumstances in which
you are talking.

The precise durations also differ from culture to culture—what is
a respectful gaze in some societies is an insolent stare in another. The
rules are not inherited, they are conventions that must be learned. Eye
contact is so significant that babies are reluctant to give it before they

learn how it is done in the community in which they find themselves. Try to look into a baby's eyes the first time you meet, and the baby will immediately look away. You will be allowed to hold a hand before you are permitted to hold a gaze.

There are other rules too—conventional rules about how close you may stand to another person, and how, where, and when you may touch them, all depending once again on the relationship between the participants, the business they are conducting, and where they are conducting it. And once again, the rules vary from culture to culture (as we often discover to our embarrassment). They must all be learned.

But whoever tried to teach us any of these things? How could they teach us, if we asked them to? How could we set about deliberately learning them for ourselves? This is all learning without awareness, without effort, without guidance or direction. Learning without knowing that we are learning, what we are learning, or what we have learned. It is learning from the classic point of view.[2]

JOINING THE SPOKEN LANGUAGE CLUB

Children are effortlessly and inconspicuously learning an average of 20 words a day even before they begin school. So effortlessly and inconspicuously, in fact, that for a long time it was assumed that infants weren't learning anything or not learning very much, and anything they might be learning was probably wrong. The view fitted with a general picture of infants being ignorant and helpless, dependent on systematic instruction and formal education.

When it was realized that children were learning a great deal about language in the first years of their lives, another explanation was invented to take credit away from them. The argument was developed—and it is still prominent today—that little actual learning is involved in early language development because language is part of everyone's biological inheritance. It's in our genes. Some experts even assert that we are all born with a universal "language acquisition device" in our brains, from which the power to produce and understand speech unfolds practically fully formed.

This is nonsense. The language we speak is not a gift; we have to learn it, every bit. It has nothing to do with our ancestry. We may have Chinese forebears back to the year dot, but if we grow up in an English-speaking community we will learn English, and we will have as much difficulty as anyone else in learning Chinese later in our lives. Grow up in a Chinese-speaking environment and we will learn Chinese; Lithuanian and we will learn Lithuanian. More than 10,000 different languages are still in use throughout the world, and any child who is born anywhere in the world (with the rare and obvious exceptions of traumatized infants who can't learn any language at all) can learn any one of those 10,000 languages.

In fact, infants don't merely learn *language*. People don't speak languages, they speak dialects. I don't know how many hundreds of thousands of dialects there are in the world, but every child who is born is capable of learning a number of them—the dialects of the communities into which the child is born.

How do infants do it? The learning is, I think, rarely deliberately accomplished; it is not particularly desired. It is a byproduct, a consequence of something else far more important—the establishment of an identity. Infants are not born knowing the person they are, no matter how unique they might seem to us. Their identity is something to be learned, and they learn it from their observation of the people around them, the company they keep, in the clubs they join, from the people they take for granted they are like. And in the process of learning who they are, they learn about language and about many other things as well.

It begins at birth. Relatives and friends surround the baby and say in effect, "Welcome, stranger. You're one of us." And the baby looks up and responds, "Hi, folks. I must be just like you." That is all it takes—one single, mutual, unqualified act of affiliation and the baby is a fully-fledged member of a spoken language club, eligible to receive all the benefits.

THE BENEFITS OF CLUBS

I employ the metaphor of a "spoken language club" to characterize the language community in which babies find themselves because the community offers babies exactly the kind of exclusive benefits or advantages that usually become available only through joining a club.

The first advantage of joining any club is that you find out what the club activities are. Before you join, what goes on in the club is a mystery, about which you can be ignorant if not misinformed. I am a member of a sailing club. Before I joined I assumed that the primary activity of the club was sailing. It wasn't until I was a member that I discovered that the closest some club members came to water was when they added a little to their whisky. Other members had a range of interests, from fiercely competitive racing to relaxed collaborative cruising. You don't need to be a particular kind of sailor to join a sailing club, you just have to identify with the other members. "You're one of us." "I'm just like you."

Language serves a number of purposes, none of which is self-evident. To say that the function of language is to communicate is a vast understatement—language can be used to create, conceal, narrate, or fabricate; to define and express oneself; and perhaps primarily, to establish relationships. And none of this is understood by infants before they join a language club; they aren't born with such knowledge and expectations. When infants join a spoken language club, established members reveal to them all the ways in which language is used, all of the things that it can do.

The second advantage of any club is that once you are a member and discover what activities are available to you, more experienced members help you to do those things that interest you. They don't *teach* you; they *help* you. There is no coercion, nor are there great expectations. No one cares how good you are (unless you choose to join a competitive team); you are simply accepted for who you are—a member of the club—and are helped to do what you are interested in doing. You gain security and confidence.

HOW OTHER MEMBERS HELP

I'll be quite specific about the advantages of joining a spoken language club. No one forces you to talk in a particular way, nor are you evaluated on how well you are doing whatever you do. You are a member of the club. Instead, other members of the club

1. *help you to say what you are trying to say,*
2. *help you to understand what you are trying to understand.*

The helping to understand is the most important part. Children don't learn to talk by practicing talking—they hear other people talking and learn to talk like them. The learning is vicarious (this is *classic* learning). They don't have to do anything themselves. Other people talk—and the child begins talking like them.

Children don't often make mistakes as they learn to talk. From time to time they will invent a word, if they don't happen to know a convenient word that they want to use, and when they do invent, adults tend to think it is cute and tell one another about it. But most of the time children are learning silently and without error because the people around them are doing the talking and making the learning possible. The learning is so facile that most of the time we are not aware of it—until the child unexpectedly says something fluently outrageous and we ask ourselves, "Where on earth did she learn to say that?" We know immediately where she learned to say it, and we decide to start having our more intimate conversations in another room.

The basic requirement for effortless and essentially error-free learning from what others do is *understanding* what they are doing. To learn to say "Look at the big dog" or "Pass the ketchup, please" it's necessary to understand what other people are talking about when they say these things. And typically, this is what grownups (and older children) do when they talk in the presence of children. They spend a great deal of time giving *commentaries* on what they are doing and on the state of the world around them.

If there is anything innate about infant language learning, it is the compulsion that adults have to talk to babies before the babies can understand them. But if adults did not do this—if they waited for children's comprehension before they conversed with them—children would never learn to talk.

Introduced to a baby, most grownups immediately start a conversation: "So how are we today? Isn't that a great hat you're wearing? Look at the big dog over there." Grownups give commentaries: "Here's your juice. Let's change those wet socks. Isn't that the neighbor's cat coming down the driveway?"

At the same time, adults rush to help babies say whatever they think the baby is trying to say. An infant says, "Waw, waw, waw" and a grownup says, "Oh, you mean 'Please may I have a cookie'."

The need of adults to engage in conversation with infants in no position to talk back to them seems so compelling that they will often borrow other people's babies to talk to, if they have none of their own. Or they'll talk to puppies and kittens.

Much of what is said around a child in the first few years of a child's life is self-explanatory. When an adult says to a child, "Here's your apple juice," it is usually obvious to the child what the adult is talking about—the adult is offering some juice. And when one adult says to another, "Here's your coffee," or, "I'll switch on the TV," it is again usually apparent what the adults are talking about.

It doesn't matter if the child misunderstands and makes a mistake of interpretation. No one knows that the child is learning in any case, and subsequent experience quickly puts the child right. And if the child has no idea about what is being said, so there is no possibility of learning, the child will quickly lose interest and turn attention elsewhere. The right to ignore anything that doesn't make sense is a crucial element of any child's learning—and the first right children are likely to lose when they get to the controlled learning environment of school.[3]

LEARNING WHO WE ARE

Vocabulary isn't all that children learn without anyone knowing about it, and without practice. They learn how to put words together into powerful statements, assertions, and demands, which they express with authority and assurance. They don't put words together randomly, unless totally confused. All children talk systematically; they use grammar.

Children may not use the grammar their parents or teachers use, but their parents and teachers probably don't use the grammar *they* think they use. And no one speaks the grammar that is formally taught in schools. That is a grammar for autopsies, for the dissection of dead language on mortuary slabs of paper.

The grammar—or rather grammars—that all people learn to speak are dynamic grammars that enable us to produce and understand the language that expresses the identity and concerns of communities of people. The grammar and vocabulary that we learn is our cohesion with the communities with whom we identify. It is the reflection of who we are.

Most children, initially at least, learn to talk like their parents, with the same characteristic nuances, emphases, and intonation patterns. But very soon all children, in addition to (or instead of) speaking like their families, begin speaking like the people who will exert a far more powerful influence on their view of themselves and the world. They start talking like their friends.

Children start talking like the people with whom they most profoundly want to identify. They do so with exquisite precision. They do not learn to talk roughly like their friends or approximately like their friends. They learn to talk *exactly* like them, as if they were cloned. We may characterize the way they talk as bizarre or uneducated or even ignorant, but they do not make mistakes. This is very precise learning—and again it is accomplished without ostensible practice or conscious intention.

None of this is a behavioristic stimulus-response theory, incidentally. I am not saying that children learn to talk like the people they hear talking most. When they get to school children hear their teachers talking 90 percent of the time, with the other 10 percent divided up among the students. But children do not end up talking like their teachers—unless they would like to become teachers themselves.

Children learn many other things from their friends. They learn appropriate ways to walk, dress, and ornament themselves. They learn what to laugh at and what to take seriously. They learn values and aspirations, and what in general they might expect from life and from the world. All of this learning they do effortlessly, too—and it becomes the solid core of who they are. It is their identity—and the basis of all their confidence in facing the world.

Parents will know how difficult it is to get six-year-olds to wear T-shirts different from the shirts their friends wear or to do their hair differently. Do you think they have been studying and practicing fashion? They learn from the company they keep.

LEARNING WHO WE ARE NOT

The continual learning we do so effortlessly and inconspicuously is not always good for us. We can learn things that impair us—and we remember these things for the rest of our lives, too.

We can't pick and choose what we learn (though we can, to a point, be selective about the company we keep; we can choose what we hope to learn.) The company we keep influences us whether we want it to or not. When people welcome us into their club or community we readily identify with them. But when people say, "You're not welcome in our club," or "You don't fit in around here," we learn that we don't belong, this is not the kind of person we are nor the kind of person we want to be.

We build our identity from the clubs we are excluded from as well as from those we join. We learn who we are as much from the people we don't want to be like as from those we do. And as we decide who we are, so we start to act those roles out.

Whether it is ultimately to our advantage or not, we become who we are from the company we keep and from the company we shun, or which shuns us.

Language gets so much attention because it is a primary way by which we establish our own identity and also the primary way by which we identify and categorize other people. It is perceived to be the core of everyone's identity. That is why one of the most offensive and destructive things that anyone can do is to try to change the way another person talks. Try to strip away people's language, and you attack the very core of their identity. Your intentions may be the best but they are mistaken and misguided. It is possible to learn more than one language— more than one dialect and particular way of viewing the world. We all do these things routinely in every club we join. But we don't do so by giving up all our emblems of affiliation in the other clubs to which we belong, certainly not in those that define most clearly who we are.

The way to change the way people talk is to make it possible for them to join new and (for them) desirable clubs, not to renounce the old and trusted ones.[4]

LEARNING CONTINUES IN SCHOOL

Children's language expansion continues effortlessly and inconspicuously after they begin school. One third-grade teacher who had heard reports of early vocabulary development wondered how many words her students would learn during the school year they were with her.

She began by estimating the size of their vocabulary (not a difficult thing to do, as I explain in the notes at the end of this book). She didn't wait around for her children to get a year older. She went to an adjacent classroom where there were fourth-grade students and estimated the size of *their* vocabulary. She then subtracted the third-grade average from the fourth-grade average and concluded, "This is approximately the number of words my students will be learning during the year they are with me."

She then divided that total by 365 (because it wasn't a leap year) and said, "This, roughly, is the number of words each of my students will be learning every day during the coming year." And the result—many people including myself have checked the teacher's arithmetic—was 27. On the average, her students would be learning *27 words a day*.

At this point you might want to question the teacher's reasoning. She divided by 365—including Saturdays, Sundays, and school holidays in her total. And she made no allowance for forgetting, counting only the words children were learning *and remembering*. Twenty seven words a day. If a child stayed in bed one day, she would have to learn 54 words the next, just to keep up.[5]

I make a point of reporting this research to teachers whenever I can, and I frequently receive vehement objection. A teacher will declare, "That must be wrong. It takes me an hour to teach 10 words on a word list, and I'm lucky if the little devils remember 5 words the next day and 2 at the end of the week. So how could children be learning 27 words a day, with no forgetting?"

And I say, "I suppose it's when they're not working on the word list."

The teacher is contrasting the consequences of the official theory that learning requires work and organization with learning as a member of the club, which is so unobtrusive that we require "research" to demonstrate that it is taking place. And even then some people will doubt it.

One group of researchers who were inclined to doubt all of these findings worked at the Center for the Study of Reading at the University of Illinois, a federally funded institution that might be said to have been dedicated to the proposition that children won't learn anything that isn't presented to them in a highly structured manner, diligently worked on, and constantly monitored.

These researchers expertly replicated and recalculated many of the studies of young children's informal vocabulary development, and to their credit they reported that they could not invalidate the general findings. They then did what might be considered a diabolical thing. They tested the vocabulary learning of high school students. Everyone knows that adolescents have other things on their minds in place of learning. Surely *they* can't still be expanding their vocabularies at such an incredible rate?[6]

Again to their credit, the researchers reported that teenagers still learn new words at an average rate of 3,400 words per year. You'd think they would run out of words. The average learning rate of all the thousands of students tested was still nearly 10 words per day, every day of the year.

Of course, 3,400 was an average. Some at the lower end of the range were learning "only" 1,500 words a year. If I'd told you at the beginning that high school students were capable of learning 1,500 new words a year, with no forgetting, you might have been incredulous and have wondered how anyone could learn that much. But these were the students at the *lower* end of the range. The ones at the other extreme were learning up to 8,500 new words a year, or well over 20 words per day. In fact, there is no indication that vocabulary learning ever stops, provided we can keep encountering new words in a comprehensible context.

Confronted by such a range, the researchers naturally wondered what made the difference. Why do some students learn "as few" as 1,500 new words a year while others learn up to 8,500? They rounded up the usual suspects—ethnic origin, socioeconomic status, parents' education, parents' occupation, family income, size of family, position in birth order—but none of these accounted for the difference. But they did find what seemed to be making the difference, possibly much to the surprise of some people but not to many others. What made the difference was *reading*, keeping the company of books.

The researchers published this as a great discovery. People who read a lot are likely to learn a large number of words. The researchers didn't find that you need a large vocabulary in order to read, or someone to teach you vocabulary while you read—all you need to become a reader is interesting materials that make sense to you. But if you read, your vocabulary will grow. The fact that you don't understand a few words doesn't matter; this is the time when you learn new words.

The researchers published other remarkable findings concerning what people learn while they read. They discovered that people who read a lot are likely to be good readers. Once again, they didn't find that you need to be a good reader in order to read a lot, but if you read a lot your reading ability increases. They discovered that people who read a lot also understand better what they read, tend to be better writers and spellers, and tend to have better academic skills. They didn't say this, but my conclusion is that if only we could encourage students to read more, it would take care of many of their problems in school.

THE ADVANTAGES OF READING

One might object that evidence that people learn so much while they are unobtrusively reading disproves the classic view that you learn from the company you keep. Where is the company if you sit alone wrapped up in a book?

But reading is not a solitary activity. Readers are never alone. Readers can join the company of the characters they read about—that is the reason we read stories of people with whom we can identify or of situations in which we would like to be. When we read, we can join any club in the world—a powerful advantage of reading.[7]

When we read we can also join the company of authors. We can share ideas and experiences with them, often in considerably more comfort and security than the authors were in when they had their ideas and experiences or wrote their books. We can also employ authors as guides to help us to learn new words, to sharpen our skills of reading and writing, and to augment our abilities in the expression of ideas, in argument, and in thinking creatively.

Reading and writing are universally claimed to be useful if not essential parts of being a good citizen and a competent and desirable worker—sometimes exaggeratedly so in my opinion. The prime value of reading and writing is the *experience* they provide through which we may constantly and unobtrusively learn.

This inevitable learning when we are in the company of printed materials is unwittingly acknowledged every time there is a call for a book to be banned from a library shelf or for a particular point of view not to be published in a newspaper or magazine. Everyone recognizes that print is potent—it's part of the classic view of learning.

Joining the Literacy Club

How do we become members of the reading and writing club? How do children—or grown ups—identify themselves as participants in the literate world?

We don't have to be skilled readers to join the literacy club nor need we know very much about writing. Quite the contrary. It is not until we are members of the literacy club that we can learn to read and to write. Literacy doesn't come as the climax of a sustained regime of reading and writing instruction to which we and our teachers have diligently applied ourselves. Reading and writing should come as effortlessly as the understanding and mastery of speech. Everything else—all the more prominent exercises, drills, corrections, and tests—are distractions and sometimes insuperable obstacles on the way to literacy.

Where learning to read and write is conspicuously not effortless, it is not because of an inability to learn but because of a personal or socio-cultural history of having learned the wrong thing. Learning that accomplishment in reading and writing is difficult or unlikely to occur (for the individual concerned) can be debilitating, disheartening, confidence sapping, and almost impossible to overcome without a sensitive and supportive collaborator, a more experienced member of the club.

We have seen that people who read a lot become good readers. The skill of reading is one of the benefits of keeping the company of authors (provided you see yourself as a member of the club). Authors have this collaborative role from the very beginning; they are the people who teach children to read. In other words, you learn to read by reading.

The fact that children learn to read by reading is well established by educational research (though largely ignored if not suppressed by the official theory that prefers the control of conspicuous effort). It is also part of the classic and common sense view that children who spend time with books, even when they are still only able to make sense of the pictures, are likely to become competent readers very soon.

This presents a conundrum to many people, however, who very reasonably ask, "If you learn to read by reading, how do you get on the merry-go-round in the first place? How can you read, in order to read, in order to learn to read?"

The question has a very simple answer. If you can't read for yourself, someone has to read for you.

You will remember the situation in the spoken language club. First someone shows you what can be done then helps with whatever you want to do yourself. Specifically, in the literacy club, someone helps you to read what you are interested in reading and helps you to write what you would like to write.

READING TO, FOR, AND WITH CHILDREN

Sometimes there is concern about spending too much time "helping children" to do something, as opposed to having them taught how to do it for themselves. Teachers, for example, might say, "If I always read to children, won't they become dependent on me, and expect me to do it all the time?"

Teachers needn't worry. There's a simple yet powerful reason why children will never become dependent upon other people to do anything they think they can do for themselves—they don't have the patience. Someone once brushed our hair for us and tied our shoelaces, but we don't expect anyone to do so now. Nor do children, who normally insist on attending to themselves long before we think they are ready to do so, testing our own patience.

Reading to children usually goes through three clear stages as children move from membership of your particular literacy club to the more general club where authors themselves are the most experienced and accessible members.

First you are *reading for* the child, who is perhaps sitting in front of you, looking at your mouth as the words come out. Then the child is beside you, sitting on your lap or looking over your shoulder, looking at the book, not at you. You're no longer reading to or for the child but *reading with* the child.

And finally comes that most frustrating moment in many parents' lives when they haven't got to the end of the page *and the child turns it over.* As British educator Margaret Meek would say, children at that point are no longer relying on a nearby adult for reading; they have trusted themselves to authors. And as Margaret Meek has also commented, it is a tragedy when many "reading teachers" stand between children and the authors who will teach them to read.[1]

THE EVER-OBLIGING AUTHOR

How do authors teach children to read? There's really no mystery about it from the classic point of view that says that you learn from the company you keep, although it is totally inexplicable from the official theory that believes learning requires effort and organized instruction.

Every time a child reads a book—especially one of those favorite stories that children enjoy hearing and reading long after they know every word by heart—the author shows the child how to read it. The same applies with those popular books from which a child can predict what the next word is likely to be. The child doesn't read the book to *learn* the story but to *enjoy* it. The story is already familiar or largely familiar. As Margaret Meek says, the child knows the words and the author shows the child how to read them—as effortlessly and inconspicuously as the child learns 20 words a day of spoken language.

It is ironic that in the situation I have just described some misguided parents or teachers may take the book away from the child because they think it is "too easy" or that the child knows the story already. This is a supreme example of the tragedy of the official theory—that people believe that learning is taking place only if there is *difficulty,* and that we can't possibly be learning if we are enjoying what we are doing. Teachers sometimes rationalize making learning unnecessarily complicated for children by saying they have to be "challenged."

Authors are the most tolerant collaborators for children, and for readers of all ages, compared with even the most indulgent of parents. Authors never object if the learner wants to experience the story 17 times in a row, or skips difficult passages, or makes occasional mistakes, or keeps going back to a particular point. Why should they? Authors may be far distant in time and space; they may even be dead. But they can demonstrate to learners how to recognize words; the meanings of words; their spellings and their grammatical relationships to other words; and the way words are organized into sentences and paragraphs, and into poetry and drama.[2]

INSIDE—OR OUTSIDE—THE LITERACY CLUB

Learners must see themselves as members of the clubs of readers and writers so that they identify with authors as they read and reread their favorite books. Or rather, what is critical is that the learners *must not* learn that they are *not* members of the literacy club. If you've learned that you don't want to be a member of the club or aren't expected to be a member, you'll probably never forget this. You'll never learn much about reading and writing.

There is compelling evidence that all children are members of some kind of literacy club—at least when they arrive in school. Research indicates that there are no homes and communities (in North America at least, and in the rest of the world as far as I have been able to ascertain) that don't have some functioning print in them. Even the trash that litters our streets and countryside has print on it. And it is all print that makes sense, that learners can recognize as a part of the community with which they identify.[3]

Where there is print in the home, the evidence is that children know what it is for, and they participate in making use of it, learning from the company they keep. If children come from a family where people read a newspaper around the kitchen table in the morning, they know about reading a newspaper around the kitchen table, and they can demonstrate what they know, holding the paper appropriately and even reciting the appropriate kind of words—even if not yet those on the page in front of them. If children come from a family where people leave each other messages on the refrigerator door, they know all about messages on the refrigerator door, and they will want to add their own.

Children in families that send birthday and greetings cards know all about greetings cards. Children know about television guides, telephone directories, commercials, and catalogs. They can make sense of much of the print on television advertisements and in malls and department stores. They are members of the club, even if they aren't very good at reading and writing for themselves. The fluency will come naturally in due course if nothing goes wrong. As with spoken language, other more experienced members of the club have shown children what written language can do and have helped them to read what they are interested in reading and to write what they are interested in writing.

And if they are not members of the literacy club by the time they get to school, it should not be impossible for their teachers to interest children in literacy club membership—though it may sometimes require a good deal of sensitivity and patience.

Unfortunately, whether members of the club or not, many children when they get to school are introduced for the first time to written language that *doesn't* make sense because it is part of the exercises and drills preferred by the official theory of learning. They may decide or be taught that the literacy club is not for them. Instead of learning to read and write, to do mathematics and science, to enjoy social studies, and to behave in thoughtful, respectful, and democratic ways, they may learn that these are areas of life beyond their interests and reach.[4]

5

Learning Through Life

We learn from the company we keep, in person and in print. We doubtless also learn from the company we keep in movies, on television, and through the Internet. But reading must be given special status because of the scope and freedom it allows the imagination.

We learn from the company we keep, throughout our lives, without effort, without awareness, and with no forgetting. People who enjoy opera and ballet are storehouses of knowledge about opera and ballet; those who read about the scandals of celebrities become walking encyclopedias of celebrity scandal, and those who are immersed in soap operas live in a world inhabited by characters in soaps.[1]

STEMMING THE TIDES OF LEARNING

I have an elderly friend who lives alone in England, filling his days watching news and sports on television and reading more news and sports coverage, with a lot of celebrity gossip, in his newspapers. When I visit him he treats me to detailed accounts of everything he has learned. He knows all the scores and the names and histories of all the players on all the teams, and what most of them are paid. He gives me his considered opinion about political events, and he warns me about what might be happening on the world's financial markets. He also regales me with more gossip about the British royal family than anyone should reasonably be subjected to.

At times I fantasize that I will resort to the official theory of learning to stem this flood of unwanted information about the private lives of the royal family. I imagine telling my friend he should work harder to learn. I'll ask him to pay greater attention to news about the royal family in future and to take extensive notes. To help his learning I'll send him frequent tests. I'll also keep a record of his scores and let him know if he is keeping up or falling behind. I'll share these scores with his friends so they can encourage him. I'll tell him he shouldn't have any great difficulty with the tests because 80 percent of people his age score very high on them. To motivate him, I might even suggest that the amount of his pension could depend upon how well he does.

I know what will happen. He'll come to hate reading about the royal family (and he'll come to hate me as well). He might even give up reading altogether. By making him self-conscious about his learning I could destroy it, together with his confidence in himself. The official theory that learning requires structure and effort has enormous destructive power.

We are learning all the time—about the world and about ourselves. We learn without knowing that we are learning and we learn without effort every moment of the day. We learn what is interesting to us (because we are members of the club) and we learn from what makes sense to us (because there is nothing to learn from what confuses us except that it is confusing).

But we are also vulnerable. We can all learn things that we might be better off not learning, that diminish our opinion of ourselves or of other people, to the detriment of the way we view ourselves and our place in the world. We don't give ourselves credit for learning because it is so effortless, nor do we recognize the damage we can suffer if we learn there are things that we *can't* do. Instead, we remember the false theory of learning that says we can learn anything at any time if we exercise sufficient discipline and employ the appropriate study methods.

LEARNING AND REMEMBERING

Occasionally we say that our problem isn't learning but remembering. We can't remember (or recall) something that we've learned. Sometimes there is semantic confusion—the words *learning* and *remembering* are often interchangeable, we may say that we have learned something or that we can remember it. That is the way language is. I could easily rewrite the previous paragraph without using the word learning at all (except for the specific reference to the official theory) or without using the word remember. And the word remember is itself ambiguous—it can mean putting something into memory (as in "I shall remember this meeting") or it can mean getting something out ("I remember our last meeting").

But there is another source of confusion. There are two kinds (or aspects) of memory, and there are two kinds of remembering,

The first kind is often called *short-term memory* or working memory. This is where we put things for a very brief period of time, such as a telephone number or some street directions. It is the place where we store the last sentence we read or the last thing we heard while we make sense of it and move on to the next. Short-term memory is very efficient and useful in some respects—we can put information into it very quickly, and it is instantly accessible. But it is also very limited—it can only hold a few things (a seven-digit telephone number is about the maximum) and they last only as long as we "rehearse" them or give them our attention. The moment we lose concentration on what is in short-term memory it is gone. If something distracts us while we try to punch in the telephone number we have to look it up again.

It is all too easy to forget what we have in short-term memory. A momentary digression of thought and we have to start again. But the facile forgetfulness that characterizes short-term memory is probably its greatest asset. It ensures that our current attention isn't clogged by what we had to attend to in the recent past. The last few things that the speaker said are erased so that we can get on with understanding what is being said at present. Imagine the din in our heads if we couldn't clear our attention of every detail of everything that has happened to us in the last hour, let alone the last day.

Short-term memory should not perhaps be called memory at all. It certainly isn't synonymous with learning. The expression "short-term" has a technological ring about it, and it only came into widespread use as "information theory" became influential in psychology in the 1950s. Earlier names for short-term memory were the "span of apprehension" or the "span of attention," and these might still be more appropriate. Short-term memory is as much as you can attend to, or grasp, at any one time. It is what you are focusing attention upon at any particular moment.

Then we have *long-term memory,* which complements short-term memory perfectly. There is no limit to the capacity of long-term memory—we don't have to forget the name of one acquaintance in order to put in the name of a new one—nor is there a limit to how long long-term memories persist. They last for as long as the human brain survives. That is one of our problems; we can't forget things that are in long-term memory. If we learn we can't sing, dance, or master a foreign language, we can't forget these things about ourselves. Long-term memory is indeed synonymous with learning—it is *growth*.

New knowledge and understandings don't enter long-term memory the way they enter short-term memory. Access to short-term memory is, as I have said, direct and immediate. To remember the telephone number just start rehearsing. But things don't go into long-term memory in quite the same way. It's more a matter of long-term memory enveloping or assimilating what is to be learned. You put something in long-term memory by finding a structure for it that already exists in your head; by making sense of it, in other words. You put the telephone number into long-term memory by associating it with a series of numbers you already know or with an historic date, your birthday, or any other kind of mnemonic you can find. You act a role, play a part, or identify with someone who is doing something and it becomes consolidated into your own neural structures; it becomes part of your identity. This learning is vicarious, a by-product of your participation in an experience. Because the learning is an elaboration of what you already know it takes place without your awareness. You are not trying to force something in but are rather reaching out to make it part of you. Long-term memory is a network put together from all your experience.

Things go into long-term memory effortlessly, or not at all. Either you learn or you don't. Or, at least, either you learn what you would like to learn, such as a particular aspect of computer operation, for example, or you learn that you *can't* do this thing, that it confuses you, and that you don't have "that kind of mind."[2]

Most of us can spell thousands of words without trouble. Research has not yet calculated how many spellings people know, as opposed to words in their spoken-language vocabulary, but I'm sure the total is similarly large. But we don't give ourselves credit for all the spelling knowledge we have because we focus on the relatively few words that we can't spell. There are always a few words—the "spelling demons"—that we all have trouble with; the words differ for each individual, of course. This is not usually because we haven't learned the correct spellings—these are the words we are constantly checking and committing to memory—but because we have learned too much. We have learned incorrect spellings as well, usually quite unconsciously. When we try to write particular words, the incorrect spellings may come to mind or the correct one *and* the incorrect ones, and we can't sort them out. Our problem is not learning but forgetting. We learn very well, all too efficiently at times, but we are very bad at forgetting no matter how hard we might try. It could be argued (though it is impossible to prove) that there is no forgetting from long-term memory, just as you can't reverse physical growth.[3]

The other reason why long-term memory might sometimes let us down is that we can't always get access to what we have learned and securely stored away. You don't pick something out of long-term memory the way you take an object from a shelf. You have to *get to it*. Because long-term memory is a network you must follow a trail to reach a particular part of it, a trail of connections among things that are related to each other. Normally this is no problem as we go about our daily lives because as long as we are not confused we are in effect following interlocked and branching pathways already established in our minds. But when we try to force the brain, to reach in and grasp something that we don't for the moment have a direct contact with, then we are quite likely to find ourselves in a maze, up against blank walls. The name, the spelling, or the thing we particularly wanted to buy at the grocery store stubbornly eludes us—though we recognize it soon enough when someone mentions it and our memory is "jogged" into awareness.

The classic view of learning is concerned almost completely with long-term memory, with how experiences and attitudes determine the kind of person we become. The official theory, on the other hand, either focuses completely on what can be retained through repetition and effort in short-term memory, or it confuses the many differences between short-term and long-term memory.

It is almost time to examine how the official theory came about, and how it came to be so powerful. First, however, I must deal with some possible objections to what I have said so far about the classic point of view.

SOME TYPICAL OBJECTIONS TO THE CLASSIC VIEW OF LEARNING

1. You say that learning is effortless and continuous. Yet I have struggled for years to learn mathematics (or music, a foreign language, or _____. Fill in the blank for yourself). No one could have been more motivated, task oriented, and conscientious than I have been, yet learning has always been minimal and transitory. Surely the classic view must be wrong and the official theory correct.

Your objection proves that the official theory of learning is wrong. Your years of wasted effort demonstrate that hard work and motivation do not guarantee learning; rather they are a sign that learning has never taken place, only small amounts of temporary memorization. For learning to take place effortlessly you must be a member of the club. And if you don't have club membership it doesn't matter how hard and how often you try to learn, you'll just be more frustrated. In fact the *harder* you try to learn, without success, the more convinced you'll become that you don't belong to the club and never will belong. You'll tell yourself, "I'm just not mathematical," or "I don't have an ear for languages," confusing the consequence of your exclusion from the club with the cause.

I don't say that you can always learn on demand, even if you are a long-established member of the relevant club. Some things *are* difficult to learn, for all of us, and even experts may find it onerous to master new material and information about their field (especially when technical articles are often poorly written). Many things take time to learn; not even the classic view asserts that you can learn everything immediately no matter how favorable the conditions. The problem when learning seems blocked is never with learning itself but with comprehending the material to be learned. The difficulty is with nonsense. Make sense of what you want to learn (preferably with the help of other people or other authors) and the learning will, over time, take care of itself. The struggle to learn—when you are a member of the club—is always a struggle to understand.

There's one other significant factor apart from comprehension. It is *confidence*. You will never learn anything you want to learn if you are not confident about your learning ability. Lack of confidence raises anxiety, induces inappropriate approaches to learning (such as rote memorization), and makes confusing what we might otherwise understand.

The official theory of learning says that we have to learn something in order to understand it. Once again, this is totally contrary to fact. We have to understand something in order to learn it. We have to make sense of it. And once again, because individuals differ in what they know, in what they are interested in, and in the way they understand things, there is no way that the official theory can cope with approaching learning through understanding.

2. You seem to have no hope for me—or for students I'm working with—if we've learned that we're not members of a club. Can't this be overcome?

With difficulty. It's much easier for people to join a club if they have never before tried and failed to join—someone just has to introduce them to club activities and support their admission. This is the way many of us became introduced to interests and pastimes that we adopted relatively late in life. An enthusiast made us aware of the club activities and helped us to participate. But it is a different matter to achieve membership of a club from which we have long been excluded, by ourselves or others, after we have learned that membership of that club is not possible or desirable for us. Remember, we don't always learn what is best for us to learn, and it's not possible to forget something deliberately once we've learned it, especially when it is something about ourselves, about our identity. If we have learned that we can't do certain things, that we are not a certain kind of person, then we won't succeed no matter how much energy we expend or how much other people exhort us. We need therapy.

I'm not being facetious. We're talking about changing the ingrained self-image of a person, and that is not accomplished through slogans, desire, reason, or even common sense. It requires a special kind of skill and patience and often great perseverance. But it can be done. Take a particularly challenging example—those adolescents who leave school with the stigma of having "reading problems" and who are convinced that reading and writing are not for them. They are not interested. Some misguided educators try to "cure" these adolescents by subjecting them to more drills, exercises, and tests—more of what has been going wrong for them for the previous 10 years or so—sometimes in even more concentrated doses, creating even more frustration and hostility.

But other educators I have met use a more subtle approach. And they intervene in just two ways. At first they focus on the learner's self-image. Students who have "failed" school literacy instruction for 10 years have *learned* that they can't read and write, that they don't want or expect to, that they are "dummies." They must be persuaded that none of these things is true, and that they are as competent (and as worthwhile) as anyone else—and they probably know a great deal about reading and writing. None of this is accomplished without skill and sensitivity in intimate personal relations. The second intervention is to make learners members of the literacy club, by engaging them in activities that they find comprehensible, interesting, and confidence-building, finding someone who will help them to read what they would like to read and to write what they would like to write.[4]

3. Your arguments only apply to privileged middle-class children. It's much harder when you have to teach children from poor or minority populations.

Teaching is frequently difficult, not because some people inherently lack learning power, but because learning always has a context and many people's social history and present circumstances can have a devastating effect on whether they can learn particular things. They have learned— they have been *taught*—that there are some things they shouldn't expect to learn. They have learned—they have been *taught*—inappropriate ways of trying to learn. And they have learned—they have been *taught*—to have little confidence in their ability to learn.

None of this is assessed in the "tests" that are supposed to evaluate what students have learned during their school years. The fact that a major commitment of time and determination may be required for some students to learn, or to be taught, doesn't mean that nothing has been learned in the past. It is a sign of a particular learning history. The way we learn doesn't vary according to social and economic circumstances. But *what* we learn—and how easy or difficult it is to learn particular things—*always* varies with circumstances. Schooling, and circumstances outside school, may result in what might be called "abused learners." It is not easy to restore confidence or hope in such students, to make up for years of social and intellectual discrimination. It is not easy to make up for years of hopelessness, learned disinterest, and anger. Yet many sensitive, dedicated, and patient teachers (formal and informal) succeed in restoring self-respect and the possibility of worthwhile learning, not by applying the official theory of learning, but by rejecting it.

4. Don't some things have to be learned by rote, such as the multiplication tables, the periodic table of chemistry, or for nursing and medical students the names of all the different parts of the body?

Possibly. But they will be learned slowly and doomed to rapid forgetting unless they are quickly attached to a framework of knowledge that we already possess; if they are made comprehensible, in other words. There are two ways in which basically arbitrary quantities of learning can be pushed into the mind and retained for longer periods. Both techniques are well known to psychologists, both academic and popular, yet they are rarely revealed to teachers.

One way to accomplish otherwise ritual learning is through *rhythm*—making music of the material to be learned, in other words. The multiplication tables are most easily memorized by making a chant out of them, almost a war dance—two twos are *four,* three twos are *six,* four twos are *eight.* . . . Humans might be considered to be "wired" for music. We remember tunes when we can't recall the words of songs (though the tune often helps to jog our memory). Sometimes we can't get tunes "out of our heads." Music, especially rhythm and meter, *makes sense* to us and can carry strings of words that otherwise would rapidly be forgotten.

The other way to remember nonsense is through *mnemonics,* by making some kind of sense out of what would otherwise be difficult to learn and remember, like "every good boy deserves favors" (or its variants) for the EGBDF lines of the treble clef notation of music. Much of what we have remembered in life has probably been through mnemonics, or through associations with things we already know or that we can make into a picture that we remember. Indeed, the more bizarre the phrase or image that we construct in order to remember something the more likely we are to remember the association. While the human brain rapidly discards nonsense, it holds on to memories that are unique or surprising.

Both music and mnemonics are ways of making sense of something to be learned so that we can relate it to something we know already. But these relations and associations are always idiosyncratic. What is memorable or amusing to you may not be appealing to me, so the connections always have to be custom-made for each individual—preferably by the individuals themselves. That is the reason that manipulative techniques of the official theory of learning rarely include either music or mnemonics.

5. You say that there is no forgetting when you learn from the company you keep. But I often have trouble remembering everyday things like names, telephone numbers, spellings, and where I have parked my car. How do you account for that?

This is partly the short-term/long-term memory problem. We think we have learned something when we have stuffed it into short-term memory, so that the name that was so much the focus of our attention at the party or the movie last night is totally inaccessible this morning. The telephone number that we promised to call—but omitted to write down or to commit to long-term memory—has inexorably gone.

But often the problem is one of long-term memory accessibility. How easily we get something out of long-term memory depends on the richness and current relevance of the memory network in which it is embedded. Incidental facts like names and numbers may not have a complex meaning to us, therefore they are very difficult to retrieve unless they have some immediate relevance, such as the name of our current dentist or our present telephone number. When they shift into our past, being "overlaid" by the name of another dentist or by our latest telephone number, they become difficult if not impossible to retrieve because we have no current connection with them. We may not have lost them, but they are well hidden.

The same applies to pictures or other images that we may store in the mind, such as the place we left our car for a couple of days in an airport parking lot. When we return, we can (usually) remember where the car is and recover it, though a couple of weeks later it will probably be quite impossible for us to recall the location. Oddly enough, things we do almost on a daily basis, such as parking a car in a supermarket lot or close to the place where we work (if we don't have a reserved location) may be much more difficult to remember. One day is much like another, and one parking spot much like another. Even if we were sufficiently aware of where we parked this morning to enter it into long-term memory, there's a possibility we'll lose that particular memory among all the others we've accumulated over the past weeks and months. It is always easier to remember the unusual or unpredictable than it is to remember everyday events, and certainly it is much easier to recall them.

The spelling difficulty is often that we find ourselves in the wrong circumstances for easy recall. We put ourselves—or find ourselves put—in a situation where we try to lever a spelling into consciousness as if it were in short-term rather than long-term memory. We can remember perfectly well when we are relaxed and let the correct memory come. But if we force ourselves to remember we may pull out all the incorrect spellings as well, and be unable to distinguish the spelling we want from the spellings that confuse us.

III
THE OFFICIAL THEORY
OF LEARNING
AND FORGETTING

6

Undermining Traditional Wisdom

Learning can be effortless, continual, permanent—and also pleasant—though it won't take place in the absence of comprehension, interest, or confidence. That is the classic view of learning and forgetting. We can learn without effort if we are interested in what we are doing (or in what someone else is doing), free from confusion, and given assistance when we seek it. All of this is something we all know implicitly, even if most of the time we don't think of it because learning in this way doesn't demand conscious attention.

So why is the official theory that learning is difficult, sporadic, often ineffectual, and rarely permanent—or pleasant—so dominant in education and in our lives? What led anyone to believe that learning was simply a matter of effort and desire? How did a theory that is both dangerous and wrong ever get off the ground?

The official theory hasn't always been so influential and ubiquitous. Some people talk about requiring children to learn on schedule in a systematic way, coerced by exercises, tests, and occasional irrelevant rewards, as "getting back to the basics." Or "restoring traditional values and methods." They talk as if the official theory has always been around and only recently been challenged by more "trendy" approaches that reflect the classic view.

But the official theory is the relative newcomer. It has been in existence for not much more than 100 years, and then only because it was deliberately invented. The official theory was not anything that anyone had ever before *noticed*. It was not even *discovered*. It was someone's notion of a good idea.

But for thousands of years before that, for as long as there has been education (which probably means as long as the human species has existed), there was only one view of learning, and that view was universal. It was, essentially, the classic understanding that you learn from the company you keep. If you want your child to grow up to be a particular kind of person, you put the child in the company of that kind of person. And if you *don't* want your child to become a particular kind of person, you do everything you can to keep the child *out of* the company of that kind of person.

I'm not saying there was no rote learning. Few students have ever escaped "cramming" or being stuffed (and expected to stuff themselves) with all manner of historical, geographical, mathematical, and alphabetical facts. Despite the poor returns, rote memorization has long been regarded as a virtue among parents, in classrooms, and in specialized "crammers' schools," many of which survive today as commercial enterprises around the fringes of public education. But rote learning was expected from students as a ritual, almost as a penance, a sign of dedication and a means of keeping the learner quiet. No one ever confused "memorization" with the way in which anyone became a particular kind of person.

COMMUNITIES FOR LEARNERS

You learn in communities of people who do what you are expected to learn. That was common sense, and it was the prevailing belief about education. If you wanted a child to become a farmer, or a farm laborer, you put the child on the land as soon as possible. If you wanted children to fish for a living, you sent them to sea. If you wanted them to have religious vocations you sent them to a convent or monastery, and if you wanted musicians you sent them to a conservatory or apprenticed them to musicians. Apprenticeships were public recognition of the classic view; people saved to *pay* for their child to have the privilege of working in the company of members of trades and crafts.

Universities followed the pattern. They were communities where scholars who *professed* a certain way of life accepted the company of young people into the *discipline* they followed. Some of the most venerable universities were places where actual or would-be aristocrats sent their sons, not in order that they should achieve great learning but so that they should become like the sons of aristocrats who were already there.

Even when education—driven by the economic demands of capitalism and the spirit of the industrial revolution—became "universal" and compulsory, it operated on the principle that you learn from the company you keep. The old one-room schoolhouse was filled with pupils of all ages from the same social stratum in the same community—untainted by contact with anyone who might be a model of anything different. The teacher was drawn from the same level of society. Teaching was an unskilled low-paid job—which usually only women could be spared for or expected to do. Teaching wasn't intended to bring great knowledge or ambition to the pupils, who were expected to remain in their pre-ordained roles in life, equipped with a few useful skills. (Sanctimonious texts and mottoes were employed as reading materials to promote the same virtues.)

The teacher's chief responsibility was to keep order among children of all ages in one, often overcrowded, classroom, while trying to implant some basics of reading, writing, and calculation. Untrained in how to do that, the teacher usually had no alternative but to enlist older students as collaborators to help to ensure that the younger ones learned at least some rudiments. There was nothing novel or unnatural about any of this. Out of school, older children were always teaching the younger ones. Those who can help those who can't—the fundamental law of any flourishing community.

No one would argue that one-room schoolhouses were exemplary in any way, but they were institutions where the classic attitude toward learning still reigned. Older children helped the younger ones, and the younger ones in turn helped those who came after them. The more adept pupils might even become teachers themselves. It was just like the world outside. Not very much came of such a system, unless there was by chance an inspiring and driven teacher. But not very much was expected. Young people were expected to learn to lead the same kind of life their parents led, taught by a teacher coming from the same kind of community, socialized to fit into the same agricultural or industrial laboring environment.

Education in the nineteenth century certainly wasn't ideal, even in what were regarded as the best schools. For most students, learning meant mindless cramming from meager materials enforced by physical abuse in overcrowded and unsanitary conditions. But the changes that were introduced from the mid–nineteenth century onward did nothing to liberate learning. Quite the reverse; the changes institutionalized new rituals of organization and control drawn from the most dubious of sources outside education.[1]

THE FIRST GREAT SOCIAL CHANGE

The classic view regards learning as a social activity. You learn from the company you keep. It would follow that the only changes that could ever make a difference in education, for better or for worse, are changes in the social climate or structure of schools, the way people relate to each other. Everything else is cosmetic and irrelevant.

But changing the relationships that teachers have with students (or that teachers and students have with each other) can make a profound difference. And the history of education in the last century and a half has been one of continual change in personal relationships among teachers and students, until we have finished up with almost no individual relationships among them at all.

One hundred and fifty years ago the official theory of learning still hadn't been thought of, but the foundations for the conditions that were to make it so formidable were already being laid. The undermining of the relationships between the teacher and the students began in the one-room schoolhouse.

The justification for change was—as it still is—*efficiency,* as defined by some external authority. People of influence thought pupils weren't learning very much during their time in school; pupils seemed to do what they liked while they were there, and their teachers didn't appear to have much control over them. There was a total lack of *organization*—and organization was what enabled western industrialization to take off in the nineteenth century. This was the age when *management,* drawing on science and technology, seemed capable of solving any problem.

There was a search for a model of what schools (and teachers and students) should be like. And one was found. The model was nothing less than the mightiest fighting machine in Europe, the Prussian army.[2]

THE PRUSSIAN CONNECTION

It was a time when many armies were rabbles, recruited—or conscripted—only when needed to fight particular battles and wars. They were usually poorly led, poorly fed, poorly paid, poorly trained, dressed in motley, undisciplined, rebellious, and ineffective. Except in one place, Prussia, which had a professional army, professionally trained and conspicuously successful.

There was no mistaking soldiers of the Prussian army on the parade ground or on the battlefield. They dressed as one, moved as one, thought as one, and confounded everyone who confronted them. They were the best drilled and most efficient army of the day—the exact opposite of the products of the schools of Europe and North America.

How did the Prussian army do it? With mechanical standardization and meticulous attention to detail. The officers didn't recruit whoever might come to hand, throw them in with a group of slightly more experienced troops, give them a weapon and some words of encouragement, and hope for the best. Instead they selected recruits of the same age, height, weight, and experience, put them into separate barracks, subjected them to remorseless discipline and drill, threw out the ones who couldn't make it, and forged a totally standardized, predictable, and reliable product—the Prussian soldier.

This was the militaristic model that invaded the one-room schoolhouse. What specifically went into the schools was—walls (or rather, barricades). Students would no longer be mixed up together, but instead they would be grouped according to age and ability, all to be treated in the same way and expected to learn together throughout their school careers, until they graduated—a standardized, predictable, and reliable product. Education still follows this basic model, segregating students who might have different experience or ability, from kindergarten right through to university (where undergraduates and graduates continue to be separated and given different treatments).[3]

There was nothing odd about this to the production-driven technology-oriented mid–nineteenth century. Precisely the same model was adopted in factories, with the minds and muscles of workers subordinated to the repetitive operations of machines. Precisely the same model was adopted in agriculture, with farm animals spending their lives in confinement sheds and hens cooped up in "batteries." Put in raw material at one end, treat it all in exactly the same way, and there will emerge at the other end a predictable and standardized product.

Numerous relics of the militaristic origins of modern educational theory survive in the language we use today. We talk of the *deployment* of resources, the *recruitment* of teachers and students, *advancing* or *withdrawing* students, *promotion* to higher grades, *drills* for learners, *strategies* for teachers, *batteries* of tests, word *attack* skills, attainment *targets, reinforcement, cohorts, campaigns* for achievement in mathematics, and *wars* against illiteracy. The fact that this language seems *natural* to us, that we have all become so accustomed to it, perfectly illustrates the insidious infiltration of militaristic thinking in education.[4]

The era of the one-room schoolhouse wasn't ended simply by the addition of a few new walls and doors, a change of language, or the employment of a new metaphor. There was a profound and enduring change in the social structure of schools. What is still called "grouping students by age and ability" really means segregating them according to inexperience and inability, as if the aim were to make it impossible for students to help or to learn from each other. This put an enormous new burden on the teacher, who became totally responsible for teaching 20, 30, or more relatively helpless pupils, unable to depend on any of them to help the others.

For the first time, students faced the problem of *keeping up* with their peers, unless they were to be stigmatized for *falling behind.* Others could complain of being *held back.* Momentous changes indeed.

And it wasn't just the physical structure of schools that was split into largely meaningless parts. So was time itself. The school day became a grid of "periods," devoted to compartmentalized aspects of learning. And the more difficulty students experienced learning something, the more likely they were to receive more fragmented and disjointed things to learn. All this was supposed to make learning easier for them, though its actual consequence was to make it more difficult. "Systematic instruction" was the systematic deprivation of experience.

All this continues today. The more difficulty teachers and students have, the more fragmentation of time, space, and subject matter is likely to be imposed on them. No wonder many teachers have begun to believe what much of the rest of the world seems to take for granted—that fragmentation is good for you. A colleague of mine at university complained when he discovered that I was talking about the subject of writing in my graduate seminar on "Foundations of Reading." "It's *my* job to teach writing," he protested. "I don't talk to the students about reading, because that's your job. Just let me get on with mine." Reading and writing were separate categories in his brain no matter how inextricably they might be integrated in real life.

ALLOCATING THE BLAME

Reorganizing the physical and social structure of schools didn't produce the dramatic results that were expected. What worked for the Prussian army wasn't working in schools. Someone must be at fault. Critical eyes fell upon the one person who was and still is blamed when educational innovations fail—the teacher.

Until the middle of the nineteenth century, good teaching was generally held to be an art. Special kinds of people were effective teachers, not practitioners of particular techniques. Now that had to change. Science had solved every problem confronting the human race, or was about to do so, and it could certainly solve the problem of education. Teaching would no longer be an art dependent upon the sensitivity and creativity of amateurs; it would become a science controlled by experts.

The ground was laid for the official theory of learning.

7

Fabricating a Theory of Learning

 substantial obstacle had to be overcome before teaching could become a science.

To have a science, you must be able to experiment, which requires making measurements and comparisons. And to be able to measure you must have something you can count. You must have *units* of whatever you study, such as meters, liters, kilograms, degrees, or volts. What could a unit of teaching or learning look like? How could there be a *scientific* theory of learning?

By an unfortunate historical coincidence the problem was solved, almost on cue, by an obscure German philosopher. Just as education began its search for a scientific theory of learning, experimental psychology found one. Strange as it may seem, education found its inspiration in the psychological laboratory.

I say "strange as it may seem." But we have become so accustomed to our current state of affairs that many people take it for granted that a psychological theory should dominate education. Many psychologists *claim* that education is their proprietorial preserve because they believe *they* are the experts who understand learning and the conditions under which it takes place. Few people today question why *psychologists,* of all people—whether they are concerned with research on animals, studies in experimental laboratories, dysfunctional behavior, or the development of "artificial intelligence" in computers (all of which are routinely used as a basis for pronouncements about how teachers should behave)—should have anything of particular merit to say about the intimate act of human learning.

49

Education did not have to anoint psychology as the source of all wisdom about human learning. Education could have turned to anthropology, whose well documented theory was that young people in every culture learn through identification and collaboration with their elders. Education could have turned to literature, whose closely reasoned argument was that you learn by encountering inspiring thoughts and models when you read. It could even have turned to farming, whose theory was that growth occurred when the most naturally beneficial nutrients and conditions were provided. All of these theories are in fact correct, both in their own domains and when applied to human learning in general. But they would not have been considered acceptable because they lacked the one essential constituent of a science—there was nothing that could be an identifiable, easily quantifiable unit.

A SOLUTION IN SEARCH OF A PROBLEM

Psychology itself had been desperately seeking something it could measure, a problem that measurement could solve. In the middle of the nineteenth century, psychology was in a period of turmoil and change, trying to establish itself as a respectable academic discipline, a science rather than an art. The antecedents of psychology lay in physiology and philosophy, one descriptive and the other reflective, neither a sound basis for the establishment of a science. At the time, psychology was primarily concerned with the nature of human emotions, a rich and complex subject, but not one that was amenable to measurement and experimentation.

And then psychology had two remarkable successes, the consequences of which still dominate "scientific" experimental psychology today. The first was that it resolved the relationship between sensation and perception, a theoretical enigma that had confounded philosophers for hundreds of years. Basically, the problem concerned what comes first, sensation (when we *feel* that something has happened to us) or perception (when we *identify* something that has happened to us). Must we first have a physical sensation of an event, which we then analyze in order to construct a perception of what has happened, such as having to be aware of a certain shape before we can say "that's a dog"? Or is it impossible to have a "raw" sensation without any mental image of what caused it?

The entire conundrum was disposed of almost at a stroke by the use of a stopwatch. Simple equipment was built and a simple experimental procedure devised to *measure* how long it took people to say that something had happened, that they had seen or heard something, and how long it took to say what had happened, what exactly they had seen or heard. All kinds of human judgments were studied, and continue to be studied, from how quickly we can recognize and distinguish colors, shapes, and sounds to how accurately we can estimate distances, temperature changes, and the separation of two needle pricks on the skin. The science of *psychophysics* was born, and for decades researchers could not identify themselves as psychologists unless they wore a white coat and carried a stopwatch and a slide rule. Today, of course, all the experimentation and calculation are done with computers.

Psychology's other great success (and even greater growth industry) involved learning. The discovery of a way to measure learning changed the character of both education and psychology. Learning, which had formerly been considered a matter of no great interest (because everyone knew that you learned from the company you keep) became central to academic psychology. The earlier concern with human emotions was pushed aside.

Aspects of psychology that could be counted and measured in some way became "scientific" and academically respectable, while the rest was regarded as dubious and subjective, relegated to realms of "clinical" or "abnormal" psychology. This is a controversy that continues today as proponents of the two psychological persuasions, experimental and clinical, anathematize each other and struggle for control of their professional organizations. In education, matters involving human emotions have become the province of "special education." Students whose feelings interfere with their learning are regarded as "handicapped" or "at risk."

A NONSENSICAL DISCOVERY

On the face of it, discovering a way to measure learning might seem improbable. People don't weigh more when they learn nor are their heads any bigger. Size of brain doesn't reveal anything about extent of experience or depth of knowledge. And what could a "unit of learning" be? A word, a phrase, a mathematical formula, an historical date, a geographical fact, or a physical skill? If any of these, how could one be compared with another?

And even if a choice were arbitrarily made, such as learning the name of the capital city of a country, how could any two people be compared? Tom has visited many of the world's capital cities and learns the name and location of new ones the moment he hears about them. Dick has never traveled and scarcely knows that different countries exist, let alone what constitutes a capital city. Harry is simply bored by it all and resents having to answer pointless questions.

How could anyone make comparisons on any aspect of learning when people are so different, especially in the two things that make learning possible for anyone (according to the classic point of view)—interest and past experience? In the revealing language of science, interest and past experience "contaminate" experiments and "invalidate" results. People who have a great interest in a topic or activity, and who have had a greater experience of it, are bound to learn more. And they ruin experiments. What experiments need is a method of *control* (another revealing piece of professional jargon) so that the learning task is fundamentally the same for everyone.

The problem of finding something for people to learn that wasn't affected by interest and past experience seemed insurmountable—until it was solved, quite suddenly and unexpectedly, by one man. We know who he is, and when and where he did it. He has been called the "father of experimental psychology," and he brought a dramatic and long-lasting change to education. His discovery was practically unique in the annals of science in that it seemed to come out of thin air, conceived by this one man alone. It was an idea with no obvious antecedents—which by itself might raise suspicion about its relevance.

The man was Hermann Ebbinghaus, an itinerant philosopher who developed an interest in scientific methodology after his military service, with the victorious Prussian army, in the Franco-Prussian war. He was a philosophy instructor at the University of Berlin in the 1880s when he announced that he had found a scientific way to study learning and forgetting.[1]

This was Ebbinghaus's world-changing revelation: *If you want to study how people learn without the involvement of interest and past experience—study how they learn nonsense.* By definition, no one is interested in anything that makes no sense to them, and by definition, nothing in past experience can help anyone learn nonsense.

Ebbinghaus's great invention was the *nonsense syllable*—a brief sound that makes no sense to anyone, the way WUG, DAX, or VOG might be meaningless to a speaker of English. It's not easy to construct nonsense because the human brain instinctively seeks to make sense of anything it encounters. And a syllable that makes no sense in one language might be a perfectly comprehensible word in another or may be reminiscent of the name of a product or the initials of an organization. But as long as people are confronted by something that truly makes no sense to them, they will learn in the same way according to Ebbinghaus's reasoning.

Ebbinghaus explained how learning should be studied scientifically. You construct a list of about 10 nonsense items (much more than that is beyond anyone's capacity to learn) and you measure how much time or how many repetitions are required for people to learn the items on the list. You let them have one look at the items, and you see how many they can recall. Then you give them a second look and test them again. And so on until they can repeat all the items correctly. When you are done, said Ebbinghaus, you will have a representation of the laws of learning.

Amazingly, after inventing the nonsense syllable Ebbinghaus shut himself up in his laboratory and experimented on himself, inventing more and more lists of meaningless materials (23,000 items in all) that he labored to learn (or rather memorize). He recorded how many repetitions or how much time it took before he could repeat them without error.

And when he was done, in effect, he came out blinking into the daylight and said, "Here are the laws of learning." Many readers will recognize the graph of Figure 7.1. The vertical scale indicates the number of items to be learned and the horizontal axis the opportunity to learn them—the amount of time allowed or number of glimpses. The resulting curve is always the same.

The curve of Figure 7.1 can be interpreted in the following way. The first two or three items are learned relatively quickly, but it takes progressively longer to learn each successive item until progress just about flattens out after 10 items. Until people reach that point, you can push them up the learning curve simply by giving them more time (or greater incentives) to work. Progress up this curve is inevitable—it applies to people of all ages, interests, and experience all over the world, provided the experiment is properly controlled and the items to be learned are truly nonsense. (If the items to be learned happen to be meaningful to some of the people experimented upon, then the learning curve will

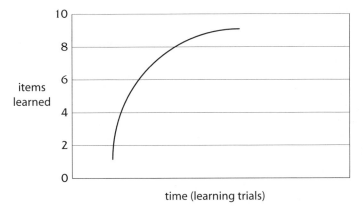

FIGURE 7.1 The learning curve.

shoot up unpredictably—20 words a day and no forgetting—and the experiment will be ruined.)

Academic psychology bought the Ebbinghaus theory lock, stock, and barrel, and education followed suit. The theory *guaranteed* learning. It became official dogma. It said that anyone could learn anything, provided they stayed long enough on task. If you don't teach something the first time, teach it again. If learners' attention flags, motivate them with incentives or threats. Learning, as one contemporary educational theorist has said, is simply "a function of time on task." Learning is a matter of effort, and if you don't learn, you haven't worked long or hard enough.[2]

TWO SIGNIFICANT OVERSIGHTS

Blinded by the advantages and precision the scientific theory of learning seemed to offer, education has constantly ignored two crucial aspects of Ebbinghaus's discovery.

The first oversight is the fact that the theory is *entirely based on nonsense*. The "laws" of learning state that learning follows this predictable and replicable course only when nonsense is involved, when there is no interest or comprehension. If there is interest and comprehension, then learning is inevitable and effortless. If there is no interest or comprehension, learning may still take place but with more difficulty, and what is also inevitably learned is that the task or subject matter is uninteresting, incomprehensible, and not something anyone would normally do.

The second oversight—totally and deliberately ignored in the training of many teachers—is that Ebbinghaus actually made two great discoveries in his research. His first was indeed the laws of learning (for nonsense) and his second was *the laws of forgetting*. And the laws of forgetting are as irrefutable as the laws of learning. I can put everything together on the same graph (Figure 7.2).

Ebbinghaus demonstrated that forgetting is inexorable and precipitous. Most forgetting occurs immediately after the last learning trial or the last rehearsal. We all know this as part of our common sense knowledge of ourselves and of the world. We know that we can cram a mass of facts and figures into our heads before an examination, but forgetting begins the moment the examination is over.

Fortunately, however, the laws of forgetting, like the laws of learning, only apply to nonsense. Anything that makes sense to us is integrated into our continually growing knowledge of ourselves and of the world, and it is never lost. It becomes part of us.

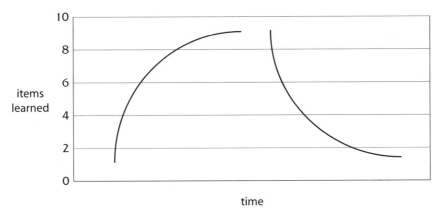

FIGURE 7.2 The learning curve and the forgetting curve.

So why did education adopt so uncritically psychology's distorted laws of learning? The most obvious answer is that people with influence outside the classroom—politicians, bureaucrats, and experts—were dazzled by the prospect of a theory of learning that not only claimed to be scientific but that also guaranteed results. To anyone who believed that teachers and students were failing because of lack of organization and effort, the scientific theory of learning was irresistible.

But a deeper motivation also played a part that is still conspicuous in the continuing controversy over education. The scientific theory of learning offered *control*. In the experimental laboratory control is essential. An experiment in which some of the "variables"—such as individual differences among people subjected to the task—are not controlled is an invalid experiment. The researcher ensures that everyone in an experimental group is in an identical condition to all the other members of the group and receives exactly the same treatment. Nothing must be allowed to disturb uniformity, which now becomes scientifically justified as well as socially desirable. Rigorous control was the key element that education adopted from laboratory theory.

Even today, over a century after the introduction of psychology's nonsense-based theory of learning into education, teachers prefer a controlled (or "structured") approach to instruction—if they don't trust students to learn. More significantly, people outside the classroom prefer a controlled (or "structured") approach to instruction if they don't trust teachers to teach.

The control aspect is so powerful that it leads many people who are influential in education—or who want to be influential—to overlook or suppress the nonsensical antecedents of the official theory of learning, to forget the complementary theory of forgetting, and to promote the official theory of learning as the only basis for organizing efficient schools.

HAVOC IN THE CLASSROOM

The importation of psychology's "scientific" theory of learning from the experimental laboratory into classrooms was so momentous that many teachers began to think and act like experimenters. I've seen old photographs of teachers wearing white laboratory coats in regular classrooms. The rituals of instruction came to be more important than the feelings and reactions of the students.

The most conspicuous changes were among classroom materials and activities. Out went complete books and participatory activities, and in came *lists*. Students were given lists of items to be memorized or rehearsed—usually not more than 10 or a dozen—exactly like subjects in the experimental laboratory. The lists were compiled in a nonsensical manner—10 spellings, 10 definitions, 10 capital cities, 10 sentences with blanks to be filled in, 10 addition or multiplication "problems." And with the lists came *scores,* the only way anyone—students, teachers, or people outside the classroom—could tell how well students were doing. People stopped talking about students' abilities and interests and started talking about their scores.

And scores (or marks, or grades) were too valuable to be discarded. Teachers were expected not just to distribute scores, but also to *keep records*. Record keeping became one of the teacher's primary functions, and the records themselves followed (and more disastrously preceded) students throughout their educational careers and into the world outside.

Application of the official theory of learning made havoc of personal relationships between teachers and their students, and among students themselves. The teacher was no longer the collaborator or even the guide. The teacher became the official in charge of work and the collector of the scores, chained like the students to standardized instructional procedures. No matter what romantic notions might persist about a teacher's relationship with students, the teacher became the manager and the student became the raw material, supposed, at the price of "failure," to comply and conform.

A new crime was introduced into the classroom. It was now possible to *cheat* in learning, either by trying to acquire marks without properly "earning" them or by helping someone else. Cooperation, which had previously been the key to learning, was driven underground. Students changed in their attitudes toward each other, shielding their "work" behind bent arms as they competed at their individualized learning.

The official theory of learning (but not the accompanying theory of forgetting) quickly gained momentum, especially when the principle was established that in the event of failure, the fault lay with the teachers, not with the theory. (After all, the theory was scientific—it had been proved in the experimental laboratory.)

Professors expounded the official theory of learning in schools of education and in professional development conferences for teachers. "Experts" published books and lobbied on behalf of the approach. Politicians used it as a justification for the massive control of teacher activities in classrooms. And publishers overwhelmed teachers with workbooks and instructional programs on every conceivable subject, an annual multibillion dollar business that became the biggest single segment of commercial publishing, with a largely captive market.

The official theory of learning spread its tentacles so rapidly that it was soon unquestioned, taken for granted as the way the world has to be. The common wisdom of the classic view of learning was suppressed. There was no possibility of learning from the company you keep because there was no company to keep, only drills and exercises. No alternative was ever mentioned or considered. Interaction among students, or between students and "outsiders," became a distraction.

Generations of children were taught in the polluted environment of the official theory of learning, and as they became parents and teachers they unwittingly helped to indoctrinate their own children. Generations have become persuaded that the only way to learn is through *work,* in the deliberate, determined, *organized* way that human subjects were expected to memorize nonsense in the experimental laboratory. The more students have failed, and the harder learning has become, the more they have believed in the theory.

PSYCHOLOGY'S DOUBLE WHAMMY

Any possibility that education might recover from the assault of the official theory of learning evaporated with a punishing right hook from psychology—the theory of behaviorism.

Stripped to its essentials, behaviorism asserts that all learning is simply the establishment of habits. These habits are bonds between particular stimuli and particular responses, created (or *conditioned*) as a result of *reinforcement*. A stimulus is any kind of external event (such as a child being shown the written word "cat") and a response is the reaction to a stimulus (such as the same child saying the word "cat"). Reinforcement is anything that makes a desired response more probable (or an undesired response less probable). Positive reinforcement, which makes a response more probable, is a reward of some kind, ranging from a pellet of food for a hungry animal to a high score, a candy, or a happy face stamp for a child. The possibility of reinforcement is supposed to be the only incentive for learning, while punishment suppresses undesired behaviors.

Elaborate sequences of "chained responses" are supposed to create complex behaviors (such as writing an essay or programming a computer) out of simple responses. And carefully contrived "schedules of reinforcement" are supposed to make learning occur when reinforcement is delayed or even indefinitely withheld. Reinforcement establishes all habits, including the habit of learning in the absence of immediate reinforcement.

None of this involves any thinking on the part of the learner. In fact, terms such as "thinking," "hoping," "expecting," "believing," and "feeling" are all derided as "mentalistic" fictions. To behaviorists there is no such thing as the mind—only connections (or *reflexes*) between stimuli and responses, established mechanically by "environmental contingencies" of reinforcement. Behaviorism is a philosophy of total external control. It has had an irresistible appeal to many politicians and administrators, especially with its clinical offshoot, *behavior modification.*

The evidence for almost all of the great superstructure of behavioristic theorization has come from studies of caged animals, including worms, crabs, rats, cats, dogs, and birds, in experimental situations with activities (such as pushing bars or pulling levers when buzzers sound or lights go on and off) that are meaningless even for the animals. When the theory is applied to humans outside the experimental laboratory, in schools for example, it routinely fails, in which case blame is attributed, naturally, to the teacher.

Behaviorism was popularized in the United States from 1915 onward by John Watson, who claimed on the basis of animal studies that he could make any child into anything he wanted, from a criminal to a judge, provided he was given absolute control of the child's experiences soon enough. After his academic career, Watson became a successful advertising executive. Behavioristic theory was augmented by Russian psychologist Ivan Pavlov, who demonstrated that dogs with their heads clamped to tables, or with surgically implanted tubes in their mouths or stomachs to collect bodily fluids, could "learn" to blink or salivate in anticipation of a rewarding or punishing stimulus.

And there was a crescendo of behaviorism from the 1930s onward with the crusading zeal of B. F. Skinner, who spent more than 40 years with teams of researchers manipulating the "schedules of reinforcement" of underweight rats and pigeons confined in "Skinner boxes," learning all kinds of tricks for the occasional reinforcement of a pellet of food. Skinner also wrote numerous books extrapolating these findings to all aspects of human learning and behavior, especially education. He saw himself as a designer of cultures.[3]

Behaviorism also inspired and justified many authors and publishers of educational materials to produce meaningless and repetitive activities that were guaranteed to teach anything through fragmentation and reinforcement. Every activity—whether on paper or on computer screens—was sugarcoated with frenzied graphics designed to seduce learners and teachers into the belief that all the effort could be "fun." Inevitably, it was all accompanied by scores and relentless record keeping.

When psychology's grotesque convictions about learning came into classrooms out went any possibility that students might learn anything about ethics, respect, loyalty, morality, honesty, charity, collaboration, compassion or care. All of these involve *values* that can only be acquired from people with whom you identify, from the company you keep. Unless learners *see* people demonstrating such values as part of their own daily lives, there is no way the values can be learned. To the extent that any of these values are officially regarded as having educational relevance they are taught as academic *subjects,* as the right answers to questions not as ways of life. The effort to teach them fails—and the usual suspects are rounded up.

In such a context, there is no point in even considering how students might acquire patience, persistence, courage, steadfastness, or hope. Or how they could fail to learn that happiness is material self-satisfaction, together with contempt for authority and helplessness in the face of it.

The stranglehold of the official theory of learning on education might still have been broken, even when supported by mindless stimulus-response behaviorism. But the exponents of the official theory found a deadly weapon in another enterprise that flourished outside education—the industry of intelligence and aptitude testing.

8

The Entry of
the Testers

The official theory of learning would never have attained its seemingly impregnable position in education without a powerful and indefatigable ally—*testing*. Like memorization, testing has become central to education. Many people, teachers included, can't imagine teaching or learning without it. "Why will students take the trouble to learn if there isn't a test?", "How will students know they are keeping up without tests?", and "How can we tell that students are learning without tests?" are frequently asked questions.

But while learning is normally inconspicuous, failure to learn can't be concealed. You don't need a test to discover whether individuals are learning, just look at their faces. If they look confused or bored, they aren't learning (or rather, all they're learning is that whatever they are doing is confusing and boring). But if they *don't* look confused or bored, if they're just getting on with whatever they're doing with interest and understanding, then you *know* they must be learning. This is one of the pivotal differences between the official and the classic attitudes toward learning. The official theory says that you are not learning unless you can be seen to be working (not working at whatever you are doing but working at learning). The classic view says that if you have to struggle to learn then something must be wrong but not with your learning ability or desire.

You also don't need a test to discover if someone is learning a particular thing—learning to read, to do mathematics, to be knowledgeable in geography or astronomy, or to be competent in carpentry or cookery. Just look at what the individual is doing. We are learning all the time, so anything we engage in we learn about—provided we are interested and not confused. Anyone reading is learning about reading. Anyone reading an historical book is learning about history. Anyone engaged in a task involving mathematics, geography, astronomy, carpentry, or cookery is learning about those things. How much they learn and what exactly they learn depends on whom they are doing these things with (a friend, a practitioner, an author) and on their perception of themselves and of what they are learning about. They are learning through *experience.*

Testing, which has become a mania in education, disregards the classic view that you can *see* whether people are learning by observing what they are doing. Instead, it is based on the odd idea that learning can only be uncovered by *probing* (watch the language again) with *test instruments,* scientifically designed and rigorously wielded. Testing, in other words, shares the same characteristics as the official theory of learning, to which it is closely related. Testing and the official theory of learning need each other. If one were to collapse, both would have to go.

THE DUBIOUS ROOTS OF TESTING

The history of testing also began in the last 20 years of the nineteenth century with the same motivation as the official theory of learning—to make a sundry assortment of endeavors look "scientific." But while the scientific approach to learning was devised to make psychology academically respectable, testing, or *mental measurement* as it was originally known, had quite different aims. One of its original purposes was to determine which people were qualified to be sent into the overcrowded Paris lunatic asylums, and which ones were qualified to remain outside. The leading figure, whose name is still attached to the best-known test of "intelligence," was Henri Binet, who was commissioned by the civic authorities in Paris to devise a scientific way of distinguishing the legally insane from the putatively sane.

In 1916, researchers at Stanford University in California published a revision of the test that Binet originally devised to determine who was fit for the lunatic asylums in Paris. As the "Stanford Binet," the test survives as a core tool of educational selectivity today.

Mental measurement also attracted people with even more questionable purposes, the eugenicists. The eugenics movement was concerned with "the improvement of the race" (no need to explain which race). The movement began in various parts of Europe and America in the 1890s when it was observed that people who were rich, famous, educated, and successful tended to have few children, while those who were poor, and presumably ignorant, tended to have large families. A little Malthusian mathematics led to the conclusion that if the poor continued to procreate as they were doing, sooner or later they would dilute the mental, moral, and physical vigor of the superior classes.

The word *eugenics* sounds Greek, but it was coined in 1883 by a wealthy English amateur scientist, Francis Galton, a half-cousin of Charles Darwin. Galton had a fixation on whether genius (including his own) was inherited. The term eugenics literally means "the production of fine offspring." The general idea was that the mass of the population should be examined to determine who might be considered worthy of procreation, while the others would be encouraged or in some cases forced to accept sterilization.

Galton is considered to be the founder of the mental testing movement. Some of the most famous names in the early history of the movement—Pearson, Spearman, and Fisher—are attached to statistical tests still widely used in psychology and education. Even better-known individuals, such as George Bernard Shaw, H. G. Wells, and Aldous Huxley, added ill-considered weight to the eugenics movement. It continues. In North America and Europe, men and women clinically diagnosed as being of low intellect still face the legal possibility of compulsory sterilization to "protect" them from the risk of producing children.[1]

THE CONSEQUENCES OF WAR

Testing did not move directly from eugenics into education, despite intense activity in psychology's experimental laboratories, nor did it immediately come into general use on a broad scale. It took a war to make testing a growth industry.

In 1917 the United States intervened in the First World War, in which millions of Europeans had engaged in mutual slaughter for three years. America's participation involved the recruitment, training, and shipping of a massive new army and its equipment to Europe. But the hasty recruitment of hundreds of thousands of untrained men presented the army with two major problems.

The first problem was to sort the new recruits into officers and other ranks. Until that time, commissions, if not directly purchased, were allocated primarily on the basis of recommendations and interviews; in other words, on personal knowledge. But who could have personal knowledge of hundreds of thousands of young men, some of whom might be an ornament in the officers' mess, but most of whom certainly would not? The second problem was to assign the rank and file into appropriate occupational categories. Who should join the cavalry or infantry? Who should be assigned to the role of gunner, cook, stretcher bearer, clerk, or one of all the other trades in the military?

Experts in statistical measurement and test construction were employed to forge the instruments that would determine rank and role in the army of new recruits. The system must have worked—the war in Europe ended a year after the United States entered. And with peace came thousands of unemployed mental testers.

But once again, education was ready to adopt principles and procedures from the military. Education in the 1920s was having its own problems with large numbers of conscripted recruits. The segregation of students into groups on the basis of age and ability and the introduction of the work ethic of the official theory of learning weren't producing the desired results. Education still needed more management and control. And a great army of testers was waiting.[2]

Mental measurers had never been reluctant to offer the benefit of their wisdom to school authorities. In the 1890s, for example, when Ebbinghaus completed his work on the official theory of learning, he turned his mind to educational tests, looking for "scientific" ways of assessing whether learning was taking place. But testing didn't hit education in force until the early 1920s. And testing in education hasn't looked back since, though there has never been evidence that it has helped anyone to learn more (though lots of people assume that such evidence must exist). And there has certainly been no evidence that testing has made schools better—in fact the constant argument of people who want more testing is that the quality of education is declining.

THE PROLIFERATION OF TESTS

Nevertheless, faith in testing continues unabated, especially outside the classroom. Since 1910, 148 standardized achievement tests for elementary schoolchildren alone have been published in the United States, and only 34 of them have gone out of print.[3] Students themselves have become so addicted to tests—particularly the students who expect to score well—that they are reluctant to read or write anything, in school or out, unless a score or a grade will be attached. Parents are so accustomed to tests that results are the primary things they are interested in at parent–teacher conferences. Politicians are so enamored of tests that the creation of new ones is the first and often the only thing they can think of when they try to fulfill reckless election promises of "improving education."

New tests are "validated" by ensuring that the children who generally score high on tests score high on the new one, while those children who generally score low on tests score low on the new one. It is predictable, of course, who the high scorers and the low scorers will be.

And students who score low on tests are discriminated against in the classroom. Low scorers are frequently segregated, given relatively more difficult tasks to perform and less time to perform them, receive less help from the teacher, and, naturally, have more and repeated experience of "failure." Teachers treat them differently, other students treat them differently, and they treat themselves differently. They are supposed to need more "structure" in their learning—a more rigidly controlled environment—when what they really need is more time, more help, or more encouragement.

If teachers receive a history of poor performance on tests before meeting the child involved (as teachers usually do), the teachers are inclined to treat anything competent that the child achieves as an exception or aberration. The opposite applies to good test performers if they happen to do something badly. Teachers tend to trust the test, not the evidence in front of their eyes. Only if the teacher knows the child before receiving test results is the teacher likely to question the tests.

Low scorers are identified as being "learning disabled" (or impaired, underprivileged, deprived, challenged, or "at risk") and regarded as educational "problems." They are labeled and discussed in terms that would be regarded as socially reprehensible and politically unacceptable if applied to any group outside the classroom.[4]

ALTERNATIVES TO TESTS

There would be no tests if people trusted their own instincts, reflecting the classic view of learning rather than depending upon the artificially contrived official theory. Or at least, the tests would be very different. Instead of looking at *how well* learners perform certain tasks, usually arbitrarily selected, the classic approach would be to look at *what* tasks the learners have opportunities to engage in and the degree of their interest and comprehension.

Out of school we know that people who engage in a particular sport, hobby, or craft are going to learn more about that sport, hobby, or craft, especially if they spend a lot of time with people who are relative experts in that particular kind of activity. If we see people bored or confused by attempts to involve them in a certain kind of activity, we know they are unlikely to learn very much about that activity, certainly very little that is positive.

We don't need to test all or any of the children in a classroom to discover whether learning is taking place. We just have to look at what is going on in that classroom. If the students are engaged in activities involving mathematics or science, or engineering, and they don't look bored or confused, we know they are learning about mathematics, science and engineering. There is nothing strange or mysterious about any of this. It is classic common sense—but it can find no place in the indifferent technology of testing.

THE TEACHING–TESTING MERRY-GO-ROUND

The official theory of learning and the prejudiced practice of achievement testing have advanced in influence together, both in education and in popular understanding. They have not done this because they have produced any discernible improvement in schools, but because they support each other. The relationship is totally circular. Testing is good because it follows the precepts of the official theory of learning, and the official theory of learning must be right because it is the basis of all the testing. At no point does either attitude get its feet on the ground, in the reality of the human brain. Memorization is emphasized, the inevitable forgetting is ignored, and no attention at all is paid to what students actually and permanently learn about themselves and education.

Social relationships among students and teachers become more and more distorted. In addition to being the keeper and giver of the scores, the teacher now *organizes* the labeling and segregation that take place within the classroom.

Schools, as well as students, are forced to be competitive, urged on by the publication of "league tables" of their performance, with no regard for particular difficulties with which "inadequate" schools, teachers, and students might have had to contend. Students themselves participate in the discriminatory attitudes and behaviors that flow from the publication of test results. Like their parents, the students believe that the domination of tests is unchallengeable, justified, and important.

And all of this is manipulated by authorities outside the classroom, who prepare and impose the learning materials and tests to which those in the classroom must adapt. Teachers and students become marionettes, manipulated by offstage puppet masters. Teachers and students have not been helped by what has happened since the inauguration of testing.

9

More Spoils of War

The development of large-scale organizational and management technology flourished during the 1930s in the armed services, business, and education. And there was a dramatic leap forward in the 1940s, when the United States again found itself participating in a European conflict. The decisive intervention again had immense repercussions in education in the years following the victory.

Once again the struggle in Europe had been going on for several years with massive losses but no definitive result until the United States became involved. And this time the major U.S. contribution was a leading role in a mammoth technological achievement—the invasion of a hostile European continent.

THE TRIUMPH OF SYSTEMS OVER PEOPLE

The Normandy landings of 1944 have been called the largest and most complex human enterprise ever undertaken. It involved the split-second integration of huge multinational armies, navies, and air forces, preceded by months of planning; training; weapons design and manufacture; troop movements; and making ready food, medical and communications materials and procedures, capped by the construction of a huge prefabricated harbor that was towed to the scene of the invasion. Apart from the unprecedented scale, much of the planning and procedures were new, and the entire operation was set up in secret. It was a gigantic endeavor, and it succeeded largely because of the application of one factor new in warfare—*logistics.*

Logistics is the science of centralized planning, the systematic organization of people and materials. It works toward the accomplishment of a single clearly defined and distant goal—one step at a time. It is the epitome of attention to detail, setting up and following predetermined plans with ruthless quality control. People no longer did things as individuals, or as communities, but as small cogs in a large system.

For a major operation such as the invasion of Europe and the conclusion of the European war, the ultimate or "terminal" objectives were broken down into smaller "en route" objectives, themselves broken down into single components of the overall plan, and then down into the contribution of every single individual in the plan, all on a precisely detailed and formulated time line. And every step along the way there was constant monitoring—tests—to ensure that everything went according to plan.

No one person knew the whole plan except in its broadest aspects, and those were only a few privileged individuals "at the top." The main task of these "leaders" was to organize the people immediately below them, whose main function was to coordinate and supervise the people below *them,* all the way down the line. The people at command headquarters, far from the factories, the reception areas, and the battlefields, not only saw the broad picture—they designed it, and they decided and designated the nature and priorities of all the intermediate objectives on the way. They were the *decision makers.* The responsibility of everyone else was *implementation;* theirs not to reason why, but to do, and (if specified in the flow chart and job specification) die.

And it worked. There were errors and inadequacies, of course, and an enormous cost in human life, but the one thing that mattered, the *plan,* was a triumph. It was the acme of what the painstaking organization of human intelligence and effort could achieve.

And after the war, still in the name of efficiency, logistics became the technological model for education. The new approach was to be detailed, centralized planning, with rigid hierarchies of control and delegated responsibilities. The "planners" were brought together at "headquarters" far from the front line. The teachers at the "battlefront" (or in "the jungle out there") became the technicians, implementers, or expediters.

Language was again the first indication that education was changing. People started to talk in logistical terms about *delivery systems, time lines,* and *quality control.* Teachers were now in *task forces,* while headquarters personnel specified the *missions* and the *targets.* Everyone was expected to spell out *objectives* that they would attain as part of the great overall design. Education became a *product,* teachers were *instructional managers,* and students the *consumers.* It was all supposed to go as smoothly as the invasion of Europe—with casualties kept to an unavoidable minimum.

Once again the effect on the social structures of schools and classrooms was devastating. Students and teachers no longer engaged in activities that they themselves determined, chose, or understood. They were to advance in the direction they were ordered, inspired by slogans such as "We Aim for Excellence." Teachers no longer set curriculums, chose materials, or selected activities. Instead their role was to *move forward* through the minefields of accountability and reporting systems. Schools became outposts of a centralized educational system.

It all fitted in neatly with the philosophies of segregation, classification, constant testing, and the official theory of learning. The entire edifice became even more monolithic, all-embracing, and impregnable. No wonder many people just took for granted that the consolidated hierarchical technological approach to education was the only game in town.

PROBLEM SOLVING

We must turn away from military history and metaphors to look at another way of thinking and talking that was injected into education at the time of the logistical revolution. The development was a combination of abstract academic inquiry and the systems approach to the organization of large-scale commercial enterprises. It involved the concept of "trouble shooting" by experts whose specialty was generalized "problem solving," the identification and rectification of problems, even though the experts might know nothing of the particular industry or institution they were dealing with. Systems as a whole were not examined for fundamental flaws (like the official theory of learning) that might explain why problems arose. Rather, problems were regarded as extraneous glitches, as bugs in the system, which could be eradicated by generic procedures.

I don't propose to examine how many of the difficulties of industry and commerce were due to specific "problems" in structures or functions, as opposed to perverse or misguided overall business and technological philosophies, values and relative attitudes toward people and profits. But the "problem solving approach" might be considered particularly inappropriate for education.

So confident are most educational specialists in the official theory of learning, and all of the organization and testing that goes with it, that they instinctively regard inadequacy or failure in the educational system as a "problem"—someone must be doing something wrong. It is typical deflection of responsibility—the patient gets sicker despite receiving the prescribed treatment, therefore the patient is to blame.

There is danger in identifying as "problems" the difficulties that teachers and students experience in meeting learning expectations. The term "problem" implies that a solution can be found, and that implementation of the solution will eliminate the problem. But instead the "solution" may aggravate the difficulties.

Many students are being taught ineffectually today, but that is not a *cause* of the inadequate learning that is supposed to be taking place but rather a *consequence* of the learning theory that drives so much of education. The problem, if there is one, is not in the classroom but in the underlying theory of the nature of learning and teaching that leads to so much inappropriate control of classrooms. The solution is not for teachers and students to do better in the circumstances that are imposed on them but for the circumstances in which teaching and learning are supposed to take place to be changed.

What is going on in classrooms may not be a problem at all, but a disaster. The difference between problems and disasters is not simply a matter of degree or of semantics.

A problem is something that can be solved, a situation that can be changed. If you are in a leaky boat you have a problem, which you solve by bailing or by patching up the leak. But if the boat is irreversibly sinking, you don't have a problem, you have a disaster. A disaster is a situation that can't be reversed; the only thing you can do about a disaster is try to escape it. The appropriate response to a disaster is not to fiddle with it, but to get out of it, to survive. The more time you spend in your boat trying to solve the problem of the leak, the less time and resources you probably have to survive the disaster of the sinking.

Much of the "problem solving" that has gone on in schools for half a century has been futile attempts to patch up a sinking ship. The only way for teachers and students to survive is to stop trying to save the system and start trying to save themselves.[1]

TO THE MOON

Massive logistical management techniques helped to bring the Second World War to an end and received a second-stage boost—resulting in another profound intervention in education—with the next international conflict. This time it was the "cold war" with the Soviet Union and, in particular, the "space war" as the United States and Russia competed to produce the best intercontinental ballistic missiles.

In the middle of the 1950s the United States had bottomless faith that it was ahead of the Soviet Union in the knowledge and technology required to launch and guide nuclear missiles on journeys from one side of the earth to the other. And then, one morning in 1957, the United States awoke to the traumatic news that the Soviet Union had launched the first earth-orbiting satellite, a crudely elaborated tin can that was actually crossing over the United States in its journey around the world—with a Russian dog named Laika inside. Even more shocking, the Soviet Union later repeated the feat with a man in the can, Lt. Juri Gagarin. This was not a problem, it was a calamity.

The United States rapidly decided to restore its technological lead and its faith in itself by establishing two great national targets for the 1960s, simultaneously proclaimed by President Kennedy. The first target was to beat Russia in the race to deliver a man to the moon (and preferably bring him back again). The second was a complete modernization and upgrading of the educational system, to be symbolized by making every child in the United States literate (the ultimate victory in the war against illiteracy).

And not only was the United States dedicated to fulfilling these two great national objectives, but it would accomplish them by use of the same invincible technology of logistics. Both targets would be achieved by detailed planning and continual quality control.

As far as the moon was concerned, the United States was successful (though not without casualties). The stars and stripes were raised—and permanently left—on the surface of the moon before the end of 1969. The assault on literacy, on the other hand, is still in progress and shows no sign of being brought to a successful conclusion, despite all the resources, materials, funds, men and women, painstakingly contrived national curriculums and tests thrown into the battle, and the enormous number of casualties produced. But none of the commanders has considered that perhaps the entire underlying ideology of the struggle—that worthwhile learning results from massive effort and organization—is fatally flawed.

Faith in the power of logistical planning to solve "problems" in education was enormous (probably the reason that readiness to admit failure was almost nonexistent). The systems engineers brought in to design the space program were recruited to design teaching materials, in reading, writing, and mathematics. Their strategy was always the same—break down the overall task into small steps on a time line and employ rigorous quality control to ensure that every segment is achieved on time.

Education mimicked every aspect of the space program (watch the language again). *Mission control* was centralized in Houston for the space program, far from the Florida launch site, and at state departments of education for schools. Large enterprises were designated as *projects,* such as Project Mercury for the space program and Project Literacy (which briefly employed me as a researcher) for education. Components were assembled separately and labeled *modules,* such as the lunar module for orbiting the moon and instructional modules for spelling and arithmetic. U.S. Assistant Secretary for Education (also the U.S. Commissioner for Education) James E. Allen, Jr. made speeches referring to the goal of making every child literate as "education's moon."[2]

Everything was broken down into small and meaningless bits. I saw it happen myself when I spent a year working at a Federal research and development laboratory in California. *Program specialists* would recruit teachers and ask them, "Tell us what it is that readers can do." The teachers would say things like "read books, understand what they read, enjoy stories, talk about them"—and all the teachers' comments were dismissed as unscientific, anecdotal, subjective, and woolly-minded. "Tell us something that readers can actually *do*—that you can see them doing," the programmers persisted. "They can identify the letters of the alphabet," the desperate teachers replied. "That's better," said the programmers. "We can teach that." And they devised detailed programs for teaching the letters of the alphabet and any other superficial aspects of reading that could be forced out of the teachers.[3]

There followed the idea that obligating children to learn the alphabet was an essential step toward making them readers, though naming letters makes no sense to children before they experience enough reading to understand the role that letters play. There followed the methodology—straight from the official theory of learning—of teaching children to recognize new words from nonsense-like lists, one at a time, a maximum of 250 words a year with inevitable forgetting, though the classic point of view had demonstrated that children were perfectly capable of learning 10 times that number, with no forgetting, in meaningful circumstances. There followed the misguided and damaging idea that readers could be constructed by forcing children to learn the "sounds of letters," one at a time, even though the practice can produce disabled readers and spellers. Hence the introduction of such gripping early-reader "stories" as *Sam the Fat Cat Sat on a Flat Mat.*

It didn't work and it has never worked, but it was a perfect system for logistical control. Part of the tragedy is that teachers themselves were recruited to produce—under careful guidance—the objectives, materials, and tests for the programs that were to undermine their professional skills and authority. The boredom and frustration to which students were then subjected carried the reassuring label "produced by teachers." All of this still goes on today, with teachers recruited to write "standards" for themselves to attain, as if teachers never had any standards before, and as if teachers themselves had concluded that the specification of formulaic objectives, targets, and standards was a necessary and critical part of doing their job.

The author of a highly successful commercial instructional program that employed all of these fragmented techniques told me why they had to be so detailed and specific—"You can't trust teachers to teach." His program was so detailed it even told teachers when to smile, and to ignore student questions if the program hadn't provided answers.

And that is the belief that has led to the proliferation of experts claiming that teaching in the future can be entrusted to computers.

10

The Official Theory Goes On-line

Today we are confronted by the possibility of the absolute control of education from outside the classroom, with unconditional surrender to the official theory of learning. We have the computer and the Internet.

Computers are securely established in every aspect of our lives, backed by formidable multinational corporations and unrelenting marketing. The demand is heard and the possibility exists that teachers *and* schools be made redundant. The ultimate crushing of the classic approach to learning will be the total elimination of direct human contact in formal education. In its place will be electronic interconnections—interpersonal relations without persons, communication without community, manipulation without man (or woman).

There will be no one for learners to identify with because all corporeal bonds will be gone. Only *image* will be left—a sound, a picture, a presence no more lasting than the flicker of a pixel. Anyone who believes that human affairs are run on nothing more substantial than the communication of information will never understand what is lost.

I'm not composing a gloomy science fiction scenario. I'm describing what is happening now. (I'm describing what is happening as I write. It will certainly be outdated, if not superseded, by the time this book is in a reader's hands.)

A FAREWELL TO TEACHERS?

The technology of electronic education is already in every school, with unremitting pressure for expansion by computer hardware and software companies, and by television and telephone corporations as well (and by many misguided parents and teachers, too). There is an insistent expectation that technology will have an even greater role in the future, indeed that we will all soon be living in the virtual reality of the electronic information age.

Two factors keep human teachers in classrooms today (in ever decreasing numbers). One factor is a vague and often unformulated belief that people are important. The other is inertia; all institutions are slow to change, for better or for worse. But not much is heard of the classic principle that people are the core of learning; technology gets all the advertising, the visual clips and the sound bites. Budgetary constraints work against teachers. There is always more money for equipment than for people. It is almost universally believed at administrative and management levels that technology is more cost effective than people, in classrooms, in offices, in the cockpits of aircraft, and in the armed services. Teachers are holding on in classrooms in the same way that horse-drawn carriages were holding on after automobiles went into mass production.

In any case, decisions that determine the future direction of education won't be made by teachers any more than decisions about support for the arts are made by artists or decisions about support for child care services are made by mothers.

WATCH THE LANGUAGE, AGAIN

Opening the classroom door to technology is a new way of talking about learning. The word *education* was once largely synonymous with experience. A trip abroad, or a weekend at camp, was supposed to make you a more educated person. Learning was what happened as a consequence of rich and varied experience, and the worst way to learn was to isolate yourself from the world and other people. This is the classic view of learning.

But today, learning and education don't mean gaining experience, they mean acquiring, storing, and retrieving information (which is what computers do). The concept of information is central for the official view of learning, information delivered raw (or predigested), to be memorized rather than experienced. I once organized a university course where experienced teachers and school administrators could jointly explore significant issues in education. A participating school superintendent complained to me, "I didn't come here to share experiences with teachers. Give me the information I'm supposed to have to get my grade, and I can get back to my work."

We live in the information age, we are told, and electronic technology is the way in which information is organized and made available. If you need to know something, ask the technology. If you are expected to learn something, submit to the technology. The technology will enable you to learn, whatever the information is that you are expected to acquire.

Anyone who believes that the acquisition of information is the way in which we learn is bound to believe that technology will be the best teacher. Everything focuses on committing to memory exactly what you are required to learn—the official point of view. Experience is relegated to the peripheral, an enticement to keep you on track, or a reward for completing the electronic course.

Pressure to remove teachers entirely from education—the ultimate mistrust of teachers—is constant and growing. And once it is accepted that students can get all the education they need electronically, it won't take long to realize that they don't have to go to school to go on-line at a terminal. They can stay at home, just as more and more people these days are expected to work at home (and be sick at home, and even be jailed at home). The two major expenses of any education system, personnel and facilities, will be removed at a stroke, while all the teaching and testing required to keep students on task will be delivered without human intervention.

THE RISE OF ARTIFICIAL INTELLIGENCE

The encroachment of computers into education is inseparable from the growth of what was once an esoteric area of systems engineering—*artificial intelligence*. It focuses on the manner in which humans can get access to all the electronic information that is available and also—though less often talked about—the way in which the electronic technology can get access to us.

All this is related to the development of "expert systems" in computers. That is, systems in which the computer is the expert, not a human being. It was quickly recognized that with all the information that people were putting on computers, even before the Internet, computers were becoming stockpiles of massive quantities of useful facts and figures. Computers contained more information about medicine than any individual physician, more about the law than any lawyer, and more about cooking than any cook. Unfortunately there was a bottleneck in getting the relevant information from the computer to the individual.

The problem was that computers and people didn't share a common language. Most people didn't know how to address computers in a manner to which computers could respond, and computers weren't capable of responding to people in a language that humans understood.

The obvious solution seemed to be to give computers all available information about grammar and vocabulary (exactly the same approach that the official theory of learning asserts is the appropriate way to teach "language skills" to children). And with computers as with children, downloading grammar and vocabulary doesn't work. The snag, for computers as for children, is that acquiring information about grammar and vocabulary is a nonsensical waste of time unless there is understanding about what is going on.

Children overcome the problem by their involvement in situations where language makes sense to them; where they can exercise their intelligence, in other words. But computers have no intelligence. They have information but no insight; memory but no judgment. The "expert systems" problem was redefined—not how to teach computers language but how to provide them with "artificial intelligence."

The strategy adopted was to forge an unnatural alliance, a marriage made in a technological netherworld. On the one side were the "students of humanity"—linguists who studied the way human languages have developed, "cognitive" psychologists and psycholinguists who studied the way people, especially children, learned and used language, and a variety of other specialists such as philosophers, anthropologists, and sociologists whose interest focused on human language, thought, and customs. On the other side were the systems engineers and computer specialists who thought primarily in terms of flowcharts and electronic networks.

When the two groups came together, a new science was born. It was given the name *cognitive science*—cognitive meaning knowledge and science, of course, meaning control.

The compact was sealed by an exchange of gifts, a nuptial agreement. The students of humanity would share with the computer analysts all their theories about human thought and language, and the computer analysts would *test all these theories about human beings on computers*. Computer simulations became the "scientific" way to verify psychological theories about human beings. Any view of human learning or thinking that couldn't be simulated on a computer (like the classic conception that you learn from the company you keep) was once more derided as subjective, fictitious, and unreliable. Only the official view that you learn what is explicitly taught passed the test of the computer programmers.[1]

A NEW PSYCHOLOGICAL THEORY

Just in time to support the intellectual shift to using computers to validate theories about human behavior, psychology came up with a refurbished theory of learning that claimed to be both contemporary and objective—exactly what cognitive science needed. In brief, psychology developed a theory of learning called *connectionism,* which asserted (through largely abstruse mathematics) that human beings learn in precisely the mindless way that computers acquire information.

Connectionism proposes that learning is simply the arithmetical sum of innumerable interconnections made in the brain to reflect the complex probabilities of events taking place in the environment. (The homespun analogy often used is that the fabric of the brain is modified by external events in the same way that a stretched sheet of rubber would be deformed if large numbers of metal balls of various sizes and weights were randomly dropped upon it. The changes in shape constitutes a "memory" of past events and a basis for reacting in the future.) Naturally, all of the complex mathematics to prove this assertion, like the testing of connectionist theory itself, was performed on computers.[2]

No less an authority than B. F. Skinner, in one of the last articles that he wrote, asserted that cognitive science was nothing more than a revival of simple behaviorism in complex technological disguise.[3]

And once more it worked—for computers. In a social transformation still in its lusty infancy, electronic engineers and analysts constructed interactive "knowledge bases" on computers. Surgeons today consult these electronic experts for information—and *directions*—about surgery, aviators about flying, brokers about investing, chefs about cooking. Push a few buttons, and the device will bake a loaf of bread. Expert systems are widely seen as more competent and dependable than their human counterparts. Pilotless flying is already a reality, and surgeonless surgery is actively contemplated.

The implications for teacherless teaching are obvious. Every imaginable educational experience can be made electronically real (a *virtual* reality) with advanced graphics and systems for tactile and even olfactory experience offered in "multimedia" packages with the ubiquitous and supposedly irresistible seduction of being *fun.* Human teachers are unnecessary when such "expert" electronic teaching systems are available. And schools and classrooms are unnecessary as well when a "learning terminal" can be available in every home. The connections are already there in the form of television and telephone cables.

Teachers and schools are regarded as no more necessary for the education of your children or yourself than tellers and banks are necessary to handle your financial transactions, or salespersons and stores for you to do your shopping. (We may *feel* that people are indispensable for all these activities—but try telling that to the accountants.)

Artificial intelligence might be considered the ultimate triumph of the official theory of learning—the assumption that reliable and effective learning can be guaranteed through the systematic management of multitudinous, fragmentary, information-acquisition events—as demonstrated, not by humans, but by computers.

Thus ends—for now—the sorry story of how the official theory of learning (and the forgotten theory of forgetting) has come to establish, maintain, and extend its stranglehold on education.

But first,

SOME TYPICAL OBJECTIONS TO CRITICISM OF THE OFFICIAL THEORY

1. Surely some children need structure and systematic instruction?

All learners need structure—but that is structure in their own minds, not in the world around them. You can't learn something unless it makes sense to *you,* however much it might make sense to other people. You can struggle to memorize something you don't understand, but forgetting is the inevitable consequence. Nonsense is the opposite of structure, the equivalent of chaos, because it is by definition unpredictable. The way people help learners to make sense of things is by being flexible—by helping them in other ways, by offering alternatives, by finding collaborators, and by protecting them from confusion and frustration. But the official theory of learning takes a confrontational approach, presents rigid barriers to those in difficulty, and then penalizes them for "failing."

The true situation is the opposite of the official theory's assertion. The learners who cope best with rigid structures and systematic instruction are those who already understand what they are doing; they make the formal system look good. These are the students who would learn under any conditions because they understand what is going on. For learners in difficulty, formal structure means the systematic deprivation of meaningful experience; they need more flexibility, not less. I'm not saying they need constant personal attention, or one-on-one help. What they need—before it is too late—is to be put into helpful and non-threatening situations where they can make sense of what is going on. They grow by becoming members of clubs, by finding new kinds of experience, and by having the pressure of *having* to learn taken off them.

2. You can't run a big class without an authoritarian structure. There is too much strain on the teacher.

This is false. The larger the class, the more difficult it is for a teacher to maintain a rigid structure. Some learners become bored because what they are expected to do is too easy; others become resentful because the situation is impossibly difficult. The teacher has to focus attention on discipline and order, and no one is interested or collaborative. This is the way that teachers burn out. The larger the class, the more important it is that students can interact with each other, engage in absorbing and collaborative activities—and take the strain off the teacher.

I'm not saying that it is good for teachers to have large classes, but I'm also not saying that smaller classes would solve all problems. The best thing is for class size to be flexible, with the number of students in the classroom—and also the number of teachers and other mentors—varying depending on the kinds of activity being engaged in.

3. You seem to imply that children shouldn't be corrected when they make mistakes in reading or writing, whether by parents or by teachers. Isn't there any place for correction?

Correction usually comes too fast and too often for most learners, impressing on them precisely what they don't know and can't do. Students of all ages learn when their spelling mistakes are corrected. What they learn is that these are the words they can't spell. They learn to avoid these words in their writing (probably because they know that trying to memorize the spelling of a word from a dictionary is not likely to result in learning the spelling). The more that students are corrected, the less they write, until eventually they are writing as little as possible, restricting themselves to the few words and constructions with which they feel most confident. They try to avoid risk. Learning to spell is too important to be discouraged in this heavy-handed way.[4]

So is there no place for correction? There's only one time when correction is worthwhile and then it is invaluable. And that's the time when the learner would be angry or distressed if the correction weren't made. Some teachers say they can't imagine students being unhappy if an error is overlooked. But all that means is that the learners must regard the writing they are engaged in simply as an exercise or a test in which they have no personal involvement beyond getting marks as high as possible. If the writing *meant* something to the learners—if it's a letter to be sent to a friend (or to a politician), a story to be published, a poster to be displayed or a menu to be placed in public view, then the writer would be most anxious *not* to have mistakes ignored but to have every error corrected. The correction of errors, in this case, could well result in *more* writing rather than less, as the learner felt empowered. It is a matter of whether the correction is seen as collaboration or as punishment.

4. My job as a teacher requires that I teach reading (or mathematics, music, or a foreign language) to students who aren't in the least interested in the subject. Don't I have to use the more systematic official approach?

Trying to force students to learn or threatening to punish them if they don't learn inevitably has the opposite effect from what you want to achieve, no matter how much pressure your teaching responsibilities put upon you.

It would be better if you could regard your job (if the official theory of learning would allow you to do so) not as the *instructor* who organizes the learning that students are supposed to do but as the *guide* who makes what we would like students to learn interesting, comprehensible, and accessible. This won't always be easy, it won't always be done on time, and sometimes it may be impossible to do at all. This is reality, whatever approach you take to learning. But there will be much less frustration, despair, and resentment on all sides even if your efforts to involve individuals in particular activities fail than if you try to enforce learning with exercises, drills, tests, slogans, and discriminatory labels.

I'm not a golfer. This doesn't arouse feelings of inadequacy or hostility in me, and I get on perfectly well with people who are golfers—because no one has ever tried to force me to become a golfer. If I ever were to become a golfer, it would be because my interest was fostered by people I could relate to who spent a lot of their time on the game. It would be a different matter if I was *required* to get out on the greens three times a week and was censured when I failed to complete an arbitrary number of holes on time.

IV
REPAIRING
THE DAMAGE

11

Liberating Our Own Learning

The world won't recover from the damage and inequities of the official theory of learning and forgetting unless there is a general change of attitude, especially among people with authority or influence in education. Changing the minds of such people will itself need a massive educational effort. And if their minds can't be changed, which will often be the case, then community and political action will be required.

I'll discuss in the final chapter the important question of how schools might be improved and how the minds of individuals who control schools might be changed. First, however, I want to consider what can be done to reduce the damage that the official theory of learning might have caused deep in our own minds. This will help us liberate our own learning and our attitudes toward teaching as well.

The official theory of learning has been doubly detrimental to the way most people approach learning. On the one hand it leads us to overlook the classic belief that the basis of all permanent learning is identification with people who are more experienced in what we would like to learn; it removes the emphasis from people to procedures. On the other hand the official theory has convinced us that learning necessitates work, so that we regard difficulty as a challenge that we must confront rather than as a warning that we should try a different approach.

We have to learn, or to persuade ourselves, that learning is not effective if we have to struggle to achieve it. The bad news is that we waste our time when we believe that high motivation and sheer determination will solve learning problems for us. The good news is that learning is most effective when we voluntarily participate in an interesting activity. We should be less puritanical, and look around for ways to enjoy what we want to learn. Unfortunately, most of us have been so corrupted by the official theory of learning that we need considerable support and guidance—if not therapy—to rid ourselves of the conviction that learning has to be an unrewarding chore.

WHAT WE CAN LEARN, AND WHAT WE CAN'T

A distinguished Russian researcher, Lev Vygotsky, had a pithy way of describing how collaboration leads to individual learning. Anything children can do with help today, he said, they will be able to do by themselves tomorrow.[1]

Vygotsky used the rather forbidding expression *zone of proximal development* for a simple but powerful concept about personal possibilities of learning. Imagine three concentric circles centered on every individual (Figure 11.1).

The inner circle, which envelops us most closely, represents everything we know and can do for ourselves, the sum of all our knowledge and competencies laid down by the experience we have had throughout life. Beyond this is the circle of things that we don't yet know or can't yet do by ourselves—but which we could understand and do if someone helped us. This is the zone of proximal development, the region where we are

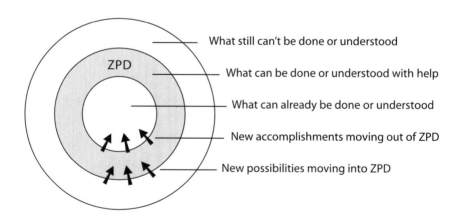

FIGURE 11.1 The zone of proximal development (ZPD).

helpless by ourselves but competent if we have assistance. And finally, beyond the zone of proximal development, is the region where we will understand nothing and accomplish nothing no matter how much help we get. It contains everything that is totally beyond our present powers.

The boundaries between the regions constantly shift, Vygotsky asserted. The mass of things we know and can do in the inner circle expands as we gain in experience. Things in the zone of proximal development, that we can accomplish if someone assists us, move into the inner circle of things we can accomplish by ourselves, and some things which have been in the region of matters totally beyond our competence, with or without assistance, move into the zone of proximal development, where we can accomplish and understand them with assistance.

Provided there is someone at hand to help us when we seek assistance with something in our zone of proximal development, then we will constantly and effortlessly increase the number of things we are capable of doing for ourselves right now and also increase the number of things we are potentially capable of doing in the future.

What Vygotsky didn't point out explicitly is that one of the things constantly in the zone of proximal development is our own self-image, including our beliefs about what we will and will not be capable of doing in the future. If someone persuades us that we are unlikely to learn something, that we are "not that kind of person," then entire areas of learning can remain in the outer reaches of the zone of things that we will never be able to accomplish, with or without assistance. We learn to erect solid and immovable walls where flexible boundaries should exist.

It is not difficult to see how learning flourishes where there is interest, confidence, and understanding and how it withers under boredom, trepidation, and confusion. We are bored when we are trapped in the confining inner circle of things we already know and can do, and we are confused when we are lost in the outer circle of things that are beyond our present capacities. Boredom, anxiety, and confusion are easy to detect in other people; they can be seen clearly on their faces. And if we learn to watch for the danger signals of boredom, anxiety, and confusion in others, we can learn not to be trapped by them ourselves.

HELPING OURSELVES BY HELPING OTHERS

It is so difficult to cleanse ourselves of the dysfunctional consequences of the official theory of learning that I don't recommend beginning with self-treatment. It is usually best to begin with other people, observing and if possible assisting their learning and learning from them as we do so. This isn't easy; I have met teachers who are liberated in the way they help their students, but are still unable to change their rigid attitudes to their own learning. As I have said, whether we follow the classic or the official view of learning in our attitudes toward other people is a question of trust. If we don't trust ourselves to learn, then we apply the official theory to ourselves, with disastrous results. But if we identify with successful learners, then we have the best hope for becoming more efficient members of the learners' club ourselves.

Try to get the opportunity to watch children in school—though not if they are immobile under remote procedural control, attending to their "work," speaking one at a time, and only to the teacher when they have received permission to do so. Observe them when they are engaged in some communal activity involving art, science, reading, writing, and just plain thinking and ingenuity. You'll see not only how children are learning about what they are ostensibly doing—learning by giving and accepting help and by mutually attacking problems—but you'll also see how they are learning collaboration, trust, self-respect, and initiative. They are learning to become citizens, members of a cohesive, caring, democratic community.

Better yet, try to be more than an observer in these learning situations, and become a participant. Don't attempt to teach anyone how to do art, science, reading, or writing, or how to behave collaboratively, respectfully, democratically, and so on, but engage in these things yourself, demonstrating how they are important to you.

You might also incidentally demonstrate that engaging in activities in which one is experienced and accomplished isn't necessarily always easy. Learning is as natural as breathing, but doing something that you have learned, or from which you will learn, may be intrinsically difficult and time consuming. Many people seem to believe that once someone has learned to write, for example, writing becomes effortless and can be done to order. But writing—or reading, cooking, gardening, computer programming, or repairing an appliance—may often be a struggle, even for an expert. Patience and effort are often required—not to force learning on ourselves, but to engage in an activity from which learning will ultimately ensue.

As you observe, or participate, don't focus on learning; focus on the task to be accomplished. The challenge should not be learning but the enterprise in which the participants are engaged—designing a building, reorganizing a room, constructing a piece of furniture, putting on a play or an opera, painting a mural, practicing a foreign language, installing a computer program, composing a menu, preparing a shopping list, planning an expedition, writing a newspaper article, or making a database. Observe the absorption, the obliviousness to the passage of time, the enjoyment and the satisfaction.

Because of the way they are trained and expected to teach, teachers often believe that it is possible for students to learn something even though the students don't understand it or aren't interested in it—provided they try hard enough, of course. But we can only learn from activities that are interesting and comprehensible to us; in other words, activities that are satisfying. If this is not the case, only inefficient rote-learning, or memorization, is available to us and forgetting is inevitable.

It is a sign of wasted effort if an activity from which students are expected to learn is not enjoyable for them. It means that they are only learning the wrong things, namely that they can't succeed in learning what they are trying to learn—and also, probably, that they don't really want to learn it in any case. I know this is hard on many teachers and parents, but the classic view of learning has to be respected—we are always learning *something*. Good intentions can't force desired learning into students, though the intentions can, if properly applied, help to create situations in which desired learning has a chance to take place.

I'm being careful to relate learning to enjoyment and satisfaction—not to fun. Many commercial instructional programs, on paper and on computer software, claim that their materials make learning FUN!!! (The verbal hyperbole is usually accompanied by lavish punctuation, exuberant typography, and—on the computer—frenzied graphics and sound, just in case anyone misses the point.)

But rather than trying to assist meaningful learning, the materials employ the concentration-grabbing techniques of cartoons and video games to ameliorate the boring triviality of drills and rote learning. They are sugar coating on the bitterness of the official theory of learning. The "fun" is usually unrelated to what the learner is supposed to be learning. It is frequently patronizing and demeaning, a misleading and exploitative incursion of the entertainment industry into education.

"Fun learning" is often the reverse of enjoyment and satisfaction, because there is nothing reflective about it. If anything is learned, it is the mindless activity, the frenzied gimmick, and the desire for a pointless and irrelevant reward.[2]

DANGER SIGNALS

Learning will advance in the classic way if learners watch out for two danger signals: (1) when they find themselves trying deliberately to memorize what they are studying or practicing, and (2) when they find themselves plowing through material and activities where they remember nothing, except that they were confused.

Paradoxically, the effort to memorize interferes with memorization because it destroys understanding. Rote memorization puts things in the wrong place, in short-term memory (where you can only hold something for as long as you continually rehearse it) rather than in long-term memory (where things are organized and retrieved on the basis of the sense they make to us). And there is no direct route from short-term to long-term memory. The way to hold something in long-term memory is to relate it to something you already know. And there is no need to worry about finding something you already know to relate the new knowledge to because that will take place automatically if you understand what you are doing. Understanding means that you are connecting what is new to what you know already. Confusion means there is no such connection.

How do you avoid deliberate memorization? Don't even think about it. Get on with enjoying what you are reading—or look around for something else that is interesting and does make sense to you. The more absorbed we are in an activity, the more we learn and the less likely we are to forget.

Confusion indicates wasted effort—or worse, that we are actually learning that we can't learn whatever it is we are studying. We shouldn't give up the moment we are confused—we should look ahead and see if something that comes later makes sense to us. But we shouldn't waste too much time on confusing material either. Confusion drives us into a memorization mode—and what is the point of memorizing something that confuses us?

Sometimes things are difficult to understand because we have confused ourselves, by following a false trail or making inappropriate connections. The antidote for that malady is reflection, ranging from a brief pause to consider what actually is going on to "sleeping on the problem" for a day or two to allow the brain time to sort things out. But all too often things are confusing because they are poorly expressed or badly written. We have difficulty comprehending them because they are essentially incomprehensible. Careful examination sometimes helps, but basically, more prior knowledge is required. This means finding out as much as we can about what we are trying to learn from another source—a different book, the Internet, a movie or video that might be relevant, or another person.

There is another resource that opens up fast tracks for learning—the power of imagination, or visualization. If we are learning a language, we can imagine conversations with other people. If we are learning about politics, or history, or biology, we can imagine participating in discussions on these topics. If learning a skill—making pottery, cooking a particular dish, playing a new piece on a musical instrument—we can imagine doing these things ourselves, and even showing someone else how to do them. Anything that stimulates our imagination and promotes our enjoyment of an activity is a green light for learning. (An enormous advantage of imagined conversations over actual ones is that we don't have to imagine other people interrupting, correcting, or embarrassing us.)[4]

There is great power in reading, which offers supreme opportunities for the imagination to work. Readers can identify with authors—and learn about reading and writing. They can also identify with characters and learn from what the characters do. The reason many of us have vocations or interests that enrich our lives is that we identified with people we met in books, who may never have existed in real life. (Television, for better or for worse, can offer similar opportunities for identification.)[5]

Many books with an educational intent include vocabulary and exercises, intruding from the official theory of learning. Don't rely on them. Reading (like learning) isn't facilitated by being made into an obstacle course. Read what you can understand. This may sometimes mean literally putting yourself in the place of children. Many of the world's great stories are translated into many languages and published in "easy" and helpfully illustrated editions, especially for children. Foreign language learning is facilitated if we can read familiar stories in the language we are trying to learn, made as simple as possible. The same applies to learning technical concepts in our own language, where the most helpful illustrated books are often produced for young people.

12

Liberating Schools and Education

Teachers sometimes ask what I think might be done to liberate schools and education from the stultifying hold of the official theory of learning. I offer a number of positive suggestions, including abolition of all of the following: tests, fragmented instructional materials and procedures, drills, memorization and recapitulation exercises, segregation into special ability groups, coercion, and time constraints.

The teachers then ask who should bring all this change about. My answer is that *they* must. Teachers shouldn't expect people outside the classroom to improve their working conditions for them; all their problems were created by people outside the classroom. Teachers must take charge of their own professional lives.

How might teachers take charge and improve what goes on in schools? I have a simple answer. They must change the world.

And when they ask how they could possibly change the world, I have another simple answer—a little bit at a time. I suggest they start with their own classrooms.

CHANGING THE WORLD

It's not necessary to throw out everything that is done in schools and to start all over again. The world isn't divided into good schools and bad schools nor into good teachers and bad teachers. In all schools, some good things are done and some bad things are done. All teachers do commendable things some of the time and lamentable things at other times. The difference lies in the proportions. Good teachers do more good things than poor teachers. What needs to be changed—in schools and in individual teachers—is the proportions.

In any case, the world doesn't have to be perfect for things to be improved. Teachers don't need perfect conditions in order to teach well. Children are remarkably adaptable in their learning—and so are many grownups—succeeding often in the most adverse conditions. But that doesn't mean that adverse conditions should be tolerated or that teachers and learners wouldn't do better if conditions were improved. Everyone, in school and out, might do better with more opportunity in schools for respect, collaboration, reflective thinking, individual initiative, wide experience, and personal interaction.

A THREE-STEP PROPOSAL

Occasionally I suggest three steps toward improving schools by changing the world a little bit at a time. I shall describe them from a teacher's point of view, but from different perspectives the three steps could be regarded as recommendations for parents, students, and anyone else with a concern for the institutions of education. The three steps involve understanding, effort, and honesty.

The first step might be termed consciousness raising, or understanding the world we live in. Teachers, parents, and students alike tend not to question the world of school because they take it for granted. It's not that they can't imagine a world without schools the way they are, but they rarely do so. If they think about it at all, they say something such as "What could we do without schools?" or "How would anyone learn?" And if they do think of change in schools, they think only of schools doing better what they do already, not that schools might do things differently. Why would we have schools if they aren't good for people? Why do what is done in schools if it doesn't promote learning? And why should anyone want to practice discrimination, repression, coercion, discouragement, and intellectual stultification, especially against children? We can become blind to what presses on us most, the way fish are supposed to know nothing of water.

Teachers often give credit and blame to the wrong things. They praise the exercises they oblige their students to work through, but not the less formal and more personal examples, encouragement, and assistance that the teachers themselves give. They may take account only of the things that are measured, in other words. Parents do the same if they praise the grammar lessons and constant corrections they remember from their own schooldays but not the teachers who encouraged them or the books and other experiences they enjoyed. We remember the things that were most conspicuous in our school lives, not necessarily the things that made desired learning happen. Often we remember the most conspicuous things because they didn't make the desired learning happen.

Teachers may be so busy concentrating on what students fail to learn from ritualistic classroom activities that they ignore what students are learning from their educational experience as a whole. Teachers attribute boredom, confusion, apathy, resentment, anger, and despair to the personality of the students, not to the dynamics of the classroom or to disruptive events that may be occurring in the students' lives. Teachers may be oblivious to the consequences of what they are doing.

How will teachers ever be able to examine critically the significance of their behavior in the classroom? They probably won't if they have no stimulus to shift them out of their habitual way of viewing their world. The solution, once again, is that learning takes place as a consequence of collaboration. Teachers should consider asking their questions and pursuing their inquiries in company with other teachers, with parents, and especially with their students. Everyone's consciousness and understanding can be raised with frank and open inquiry, not to reach conventional or "right" answers, but to reveal the underlying dynamics of every aspect of school activity, social and emotional as well as intellectual.

The first step, in short, is for teachers to uncover the consequences of what they do; what things are good, and what things are not. The second step is to do more of the productive things, and less of the others. This is easier to say than do; it usually demands courage and encouragement. Teachers who try to change will often run counter to the established practices of their school and entrenched beliefs of their colleagues—and of parents and others outside school. They may also encounter resistance from their students, of all ages, who become anxious if the teacher is not following an expected ritual. Once again, teachers will need to have and to provide support. Introducing change is best done collaboratively.[1]

But teachers still won't be able to do everything that's good. They can't make a perfect world for their students, so the third step is necessary. This is the step that could be taken immediately with every student in every educational institution, whatever the prevailing conditions. Teachers could be honest with their students. This is the only sure way of repelling and perhaps ultimately eradicating the official theory of learning and all the unnatural practices that it fosters and sustains.

Most students believe that everything that goes on in school must be good for them. They assimilate the official theory of learning and then help to maintain it, like victims promoting the virtues of a plague. Learning is a matter of trust, and many students trust teachers and trust schools, even when they are in conflict with them and when teachers and schools engage in the most incomprehensible and discriminatory practices. Students who do well are inclined to think that all of their educational experience was good for them. Students who do poorly are inclined and encouraged to believe that "failure" reflects their own inadequacies.

Students could be told if they have been given an activity to keep them occupied so that the teachers can get on with something else. (This is no problem for younger children out of school, who are frequently encouraged to engage in some mindless activity—or parked in front of television—because their parents would like a little peace and quiet.) The problem in school is that trivial diversions are regarded as something important, especially when the meaningless activities carry "correct answers" and scores. Students could also be enlightened when a teacher acknowledges that a demand for silence, or immobility, or an abrupt move from one activity to another, is not because these things are good for the students or for learning, but because they are compelled by the way the school is organized.

Teachers could tell students that the only reason they are given particular tests—and why a large part of the school day might be contorted toward these tests—is that they are imposed by bureaucrats or politicians far from the classroom with a mania for numbers. Teachers could tell students that every trivial test they take should be stamped with a warning from the surgeon-general: "Taking this test seriously could be dangerous to your mental health." The history of education that I outlined in the previous section has led to schools being difficult places in which to teach and to learn. Once teachers, parents, and students of all ages become aware of this, attitudes toward school, and toward teaching and learning, become more realistic and more productive.

One thing rarely taught in school is the sociology of education. Students rarely learn the historical, political, and bureaucratic reasons that schools have developed into the kinds of institution they are. (And I am including colleges and universities in this critique. Some of the worst teaching practices and learning conditions I have encountered have been in institutions of so-called "higher learning," especially in schools of education where teachers themselves are taught.) The difference between the classic and official visions of learning is never part of the formal curriculum.

Yet none of this is difficult to understand for anyone open to seeing the world the way it really is. I have talked to primary grade students about the fluent and inconspicuous way they learned about language and about the world—and about how boredom and confusion can interfere with learning—and they understood exactly what I was talking about. Teachers can do the same thing even more effectively because they know the students to whom they are talking, and they can relate personal examples to them. High school students made aware of the official theory of learning may show more positive reactions than their teachers do (perhaps because they have more independence of thought and less guilt).

Being honest with students can be helpful to teachers as well in bringing about a realization of the costs and consequences of the official theory of learning. (We are back to step one.) Consciousness raising will not immediately eliminate everything that is wrong with schools, but it will make it easier and less traumatic for everyone to survive in them.

A CHANGE OF LANGUAGE AND ATTITUDE

Teachers and parents often ask how it would be possible to know whether students were learning if they weren't tested. They speak from the misguided supposition that there might be times when students aren't learning anything. (Like the principal who sees all the students in the reading class immersed in magazines and newspapers and asks, "Isn't anyone doing any work here?") The question should never be "Are the students learning?" but always "What are the students learning?" The answer is found not by testing the students but by looking at what they are doing and how they are doing it.

I would (if I could) propose a radical change to the way we talk about schools. Abolish the words *learning* and *teaching* altogether, and talk instead about *doing*. Teachers may think they are teaching a skill or a subject, and students may think they are learning it, but what the students are actually learning can be another matter altogether. One thing is clear from the classic view—that people always learn from what they are doing. If they are doing something worthwhile they are learning something worthwhile. If they are engaged in a boring, confusing, or irrelevant activity, then they are learning something that is boring, confusing, or irrelevant. If they feel helpless and angry, then they are learning helplessness and anger.

Curriculum planners are hopelessly optimistic and impractical when they say students should learn respect, initiative, enterprise, and critical thought, and then list these "subjects" on the curriculum for teachers to teach. The issues would be clearer and chances of success much higher if the planners declared that students should experience (or observe, or participate in) respect, initiative, enterprise, and critical thought.

Anyone who is reading is learning more about reading, and anyone who is absorbed in mathematics, history, gardening, or deep sea diving is learning more about those subjects and activities. By focusing on "teaching" and "learning," we may see only the mechanical aspects of instruction in terms of the official theory of learning and overlook essential aspects of the situation that may be written on students' faces and in their attitudes and behavior.

Parents are always sensitive to what their children are up to out of school because parents know—the classic point of view—that their children learn from every situation they are in. Only the blindness of the official theory of learning could persuade people that this is not the way we should judge what students are learning in school.

CHANGING OTHER PEOPLE'S MINDS

For some teachers and administrators, the alternative to a rigidly structured classroom is chaos. They think the opposite of the rigor and control of the official theory of learning is students "doing what they like" and learning nothing.

But they are wrong. No one is suggesting that teachers give up their responsibility for what students should learn. The classic point of view puts greater responsibility on teachers, since it asserts that their behavior and attitudes determine what students learn and what students think and feel as well. And the doubters are wrong in thinking that chaos is the inevitable consequence of relaxed control. Students, like teachers, exhibit more responsibility when more is given to them; they take the tasks they are engaged in more seriously and experience far greater satisfaction. Teachers report that collaborative classrooms and interesting enterprises make their lives easier, not more difficult. The teachers who burn out are the ones who want to control everything that goes on in their classrooms. They don't need persuasion, they need reassurance.

Teachers often object that it would be much easier for them to change the world if they could get a little more support from other people, particularly from their principal but also from other teachers at their school and, where appropriate, from the parents of the students that they teach. Some more enthusiastic teachers would actually like to change the minds of some of these people. They ply the doubters with arguments and documentation, and they wonder why it is so difficult to get them to change their habits and their attitudes.

At one time I used to say that the problem was ignorance, the widespread repercussions of the official theory of learning, and that the only solution would be education, for which teachers would be responsible, of course. I said it was probably more important for teachers to teach people outside their classroom—their colleagues, principals, and parents—while the learning of their students could take care of itself.

I still believe this is largely true, but there are few teachers and administrators today who haven't heard something about alternative approaches to instruction, sometimes (and often misleadingly) called "whole language," "process writing," "child-centered learning," or "progressive education." (Whenever a label is put to an approach it leads to simplification, misinterpretation, and confusion. Teachers may say or believe they are doing something implied by the label when they aren't.) The difficulty in getting many teachers—or their administrators—to change their attitudes and their ways is not that they are ignorant, but that they are insecure. They are afraid their world will fall apart if they give up any of their power or claim their independence.

Administrators may feel they have even more to lose than teachers. The only way administrators can demonstrate their authority is by demanding a steady stream of numbers. They may require even more reassurance that they are not taking a grave risk by relaxing control.

The solution for both teachers and administrators is the same—to invite them into liberated classrooms, not as observers but as participants. After a certain point, arguments only make people dig in their heels. Written submissions often have a harsher fate—they are filed away and forgotten or sent on to oblivion in the world of committees. But it is difficult to ignore an activity in which you participate. Doubters can learn from participation as much as anyone else, even if it takes them longer.

The same applies to parents. It is almost impossible for teachers to be convincing and reassuring at parent–teacher conferences or by inviting parents into empty classrooms to inspect their children's "work." Parents who think a child's learning can be gauged by grades need educating, but what eventually will persuade them is actually seeing what their child can do, while the child is doing it.

EDUCATION IN AN IMPERFECT WORLD

Of course, not everyone will be persuaded. No one can promise teachers, or students, a perfect world.

Some teachers will need retraining; some will need replacing. Both, ideally, should be done by and with their colleagues; other teachers. Forcing teachers to teach in a particular way won't help—that is the approach of the official theory. Teachers have to understand how to function in a liberated educational climate. Many teachers want and need only authority and encouragement. And these are the ones who can help to change other teachers.

When I talk with teachers anxious to liberate their own classrooms from the official theory of learning, I suggest they should try to bring administrators and parents around to viewing the world the way they do. But if they fail, I recommend that they press ahead without the support of administrators and parents. Their first responsibility is to the students.

This may sound like reckless advice, but I should admit the other side of the picture. Sometimes I talk with administrators and parents already aware of the riches of the classic vision of learning and the inadequacy of the official version. Sometimes they view their problem as a teacher who is unwilling to change, who insists on a rigidly structured classroom and all the callous machinery of control.

In this case, I put the argument the other way. I propose that it is up to the administrator or parent to change the teacher, and I provide the same advice about how this might be achieved—by collaboration and support rather than by confrontation. But if this fails, I add, they might consider trying to bring about change despite the teacher.

Parents can sometimes work around teachers by putting pressure directly on principals, on trustees and other administrators, and on politicians. The higher ranks in education are often more ready to listen to parents than to teachers.

I acknowledge the conflict here, with teachers striving to circumvent obdurate parents or administrators, and parents or administrators endeavoring to bypass obstructive teachers. No group has a monopoly on wisdom or ignorance. The greatest enemy of the classic view of learning is passivity, and I see no problem with a dialectic.

My faith is that the classic view will prevail if sufficiently demonstrated and reflected upon. The classic vision is neither old-fashioned nor outdated. It respects the challenges to learning of the modern world far better than the puritanical Victorian myths of the official theory.

It may be objected that teachers aren't totally helpless and ineffectual. Can't they just close their doors and do what they know is more appropriate for their students? I have met many teachers who do precisely that—who know better than all of the authorities outside the classroom (and know they know better), and who do their best to protect themselves and their students from the worst excesses of the official theory of learning. These teachers get results.

But to say that even such teachers and their students can be unaffected by the general environment of education is like saying that health-conscious individuals can safely swim in polluted water. No one escapes the second-hand smoke of the official theory of learning. And the contamination is so pervasive, like an invisible cloud of pollution hanging over an oblivious city, that many teachers don't even suspect its existence. They don't question it. They actually go along with it, helping in their goodwill and professional enthusiasm to propagate the system that undermines them.

The official theory of learning deserves to be exposed as the myth that it is to ensure that it doesn't gain the credence and unwarranted respect of more generations of students.[2]

SOME FINAL OBJECTIONS

1. What would take the place of all the programs, materials, and tests you don't like? Should teachers do nothing? Should students just be allowed to goof off?

Teachers aren't doing nothing when they respect the classic view of learning and neither are the students. Some theory of innate wickedness seems to underlie objections such as this—that the natural preference of teachers would be not to teach and the natural preference of learners would be not to learn. Teaching and learning aren't aversive activities that people by nature want to avoid. What is universally unpalatable is the mindless "work" in schools that gets in the way of sensible teaching and learning.

If pointless and time-consuming programs, drills, and tests were taken away, teachers could be free to get on with the kinds of activity that promote permanent and worthwhile learning—providing and arranging demonstrations of interesting and satisfying ways of life, and ensuring that they are accessible to everyone. Teachers could bring students into constant contact with people from whom they can learn, inside the classroom and outside.

I'm not saying all this would just happen. It would be the responsibility of teachers to ensure that opportunities to engage in interesting and productive activities are always available. Schools should be places where students—and everyone else for that matter—can find opportunities to learn everything that is worthwhile in the world outside (the emphasis on the doing, not on the teaching). That is the whole point of schools, not to deprive students of experience but to provide enriched opportunities. Teachers who can't do their job without instructional procedures, materials, and goals designed by people who have no contact with their students are in the wrong occupation and should perhaps be called technicians rather than teachers. Many people can teach—even people who have had no formal teaching education—provided they can demonstrate commitment to a satisfying and absorbing activity, and they have the patience and sensitivity to share their involvement with someone who is not as experienced as they are.

2. Your criticism of segregation suggests that handicapped students and slow learners should be integrated into regular classrooms. Wouldn't that be unfair to everyone?

What is unfair to everyone is to segregate students on the basis of their abilities. Students who are not "handicapped" never learn to live with the students who are, and the students who are handicapped lose the opportunity to learn to live with people who are not so challenged. We are all learning all the time—and what students learn from regimes of exclusion and segregation is attitudes and techniques of exclusion and segregation.

Of course, total integration is difficult, if not impossible, for teachers working as isolated individuals wholly responsible for getting a roomful of uninterested students through a prescribed program of instruction. But individual teachers should never be in this position. The "specialists" and special assistants who work with children who are "challenged" (or who are "gifted," for that matter) should be in the integrated classroom with everyone else. Teacher-student ratios should not be an issue. The space-and-time barriers of walls and lesson plans should be sufficiently flexible that everyone can participate in making every school into a community, where no one needs to be more privileged than others because everyone shares the same opportunities and responsibilities.

A classroom that can't cope with students of different mental, physical, and cultural abilities is a microcosm of a society that doesn't respect such differences. The fault lies with the classroom or the school, not with the individuals who "don't fit." The solution lies in changing the school and in changing attitudes, not in promoting and expanding difficulties through discriminatory and undemocratic bureaucratic procedures. Segregating individuals who are different in particular ways is not required because of the nature of people or of teaching and learning, it is required by the mindlessness and heartlessness of the official theory of learning.

3. What about incompetent teachers? Shouldn't they be subject to outside control?

The wrong people sometimes become teachers. A flaw in most teacher education programs is that they don't permit students to learn about teaching from experience before they invest large amounts of time, money, and effort in their studies. If teachers themselves were permitted to learn from experience—by joining communities of teachers and learners (schools, in other words) as apprentice members—the ones who are uncomfortable without external guidance and rigid control might decide that perhaps they shouldn't be members of the teachers' club after all.

The wrong people often also become administrators, especially those who discover too late that they don't like teaching and rather than trying to work their way out decide instead to work their way up.

The retraining and replacement of poor teachers should be the collegial responsibility of all teachers, guided but not directed by parents and supervisory administrators. The premise of the objection is fallacious. External control, detailed procedures, and constant monitoring don't make poor teachers better ones.

4. Surely tests and examinations are necessary? Would you let an unqualified surgeon operate on you?

There can't be any fundamental objection to examinations that license individuals to enter particular occupations or to enter university—though even these examinations are often designed for ease of administration and scoring than for impartiality and relevance.

But people have a choice about whether they want to enter particular occupations or go to university. No one could say that the entry examinations were imposed on them. Children and young people have no choice about attending school, and the constant testing is not designed to give them entrance to particular occupations, only to keep them under control and to manipulate their everyday experiences.

It can't be argued that all of the competitiveness and trivial tests are designed to prepare students for the competitive examinations they might encounter later in life. Many of them will never meet such challenges. And in any case, unremitting experience of competitiveness, apprehension, and triviality doesn't strengthen students for future trials and adversity. The people best able to survive sudden starvation are those who have been well fed, not starved for most of their life. Life is rarely as competitive and undeviatingly challenging outside school as it is inside.

5. What would your ideal school be like?

This is a frequent question, but I doubt whether "ideal schools" are either possible or necessary. There could never be a formula for a worthwhile school. The whole point about schools liberated from the official theory of learning is that they wouldn't be standardized. They would come in a variety of guises.   .

The essence of any liberated school is that it would be a community—not a hierarchy of principal, teachers, support staff, and students but a place where people gather to engage in interesting activities. Teachers, students, and everyone else in the school would be partners in a collaborative of initiative and enterprise. There would probably be more teachers, too—better paid and more experienced—and more assistant and apprentice teachers as well.

There are some things that all liberated schools would *lack* in common—there would be an absence of mindless exercises, punitive tests, discrimination, segregation, pointless competition, labeling of individuals, restrictive timetables, and public and private humiliation of teachers and students.

Other things however they would all have in common. There would be opportunities for everyone to engage in interesting activities. There would be many interesting activities to engage in, from anthropology to zoology. There would be many interesting people around to demonstrate interesting pursuits and to assist interested learners to engage in them. There would be possibilities for everyone with particular interests and talents to get access to the highest levels of participation. Schools full of clubs, in other words. Not all schools would attempt to do the same things; each would do what it was best at. Schools would vary the way individuals vary.

I've never seen an ideal school, but I've visited many schools with enlightened and enthusiastic administrators encouraging liberated teachers in liberated classrooms. And as I've tried to emphasize, good teachers abound, to the extent that they are able to escape the narrow thinking and destructive interventions of the official theory of learning.

Teachers are at the core, obviously. Not just the formal teachers on the payroll but anyone from whom anyone else can learn. But the appointed staff of the school have a prime responsibility because it is their job to ensure all the discoveries, contacts, and collaboration have a chance to take place. In other words, their responsibility is organization. Not hierarchical organization from the top, but community organization, reaching outward.

All the good teachers I have known have been good organizers, arranging interesting experiences for their students and themselves, and protecting those experiences from officious interference.

There is no shortage of good organizers in the world—though it is interesting how few of them make their way up through bureaucracies. I'm not talking about people with diplomas in management skills or in leadership and motivation. I'm talking about people with the talent and determination to make interesting possibilities occur in a creative and productive way.

Many teachers are good organizers, though not all by any means, and so are many people in music, drama, ballet and sports, in hospitals and doctors' offices, in travel agencies and taxi services, at home with their children, and in clubs of all kinds. Like the best leaders, the best organizers are not necessarily found in positions where they claim their responsibilities to be planning, budgeting, and telling other people what to do. Leaders and organizers can arise all over the place.

Some people have the remarkable talent and dedication to be able to organize good conferences. I mention this because I want to draw a moral from it.

I go to a lot of professional conferences. Some are a delight, though others are not. This is how a good conference is organized:

There is always plenty going on—speakers, displays, discussions, excursions, and cultural events. There are also constant possibilities for escape, for rest, reflection, conversation, reading, and writing. There are quiet corners; facilities for exercise; access to food, drink, and bathrooms; and opportunities for self- and social expression, with no coercion or evaluation. Full rein is given to the classic vision of learning, and no one even considers the rituals of the official theory. A civilized experience, in other words, different perhaps for every participant but rewarding and satisfying for all.

That is one image of a liberated school.[3]

Notes

CHAPTER 1: A TALE OF TWO VISIONS

1. The constant call to improve education by "getting back to basics"—meaning more standardization of instruction, more centralized control of teaching, and more testing and accountability—is one of the few things that political parties of the right and the left seem to agree upon. Such is the power of the official theory of learning. The classic point of view is rarely formally considered, although its principles that learning largely takes place at social and emotional levels through personal identification and group affiliation are inevitably exploited in political debate and electioneering.

CHAPTER 2: A QUESTION OF IDENTITY

1. Margaret Mead (1976), in her classic anthropological studies in New Guinea, reports that children quickly learn to engage in activities they see their parents enjoying and equally quickly learn that routine activities their parents do not enjoy are not enjoyable.

2. My club membership analogy cloaks a number of highly charged issues, including concerns of minority groups, language differences, and, inevitably, politics. In a small and useful handbook of linguistic ethnography, Gumperz (1982) provides many examples of how language interactions vary according to the social and ethnic backgrounds of the people involved and according to their gender. Many chapters in the book exemplify how language development and world views depend on who belongs in a group—and who doesn't. In an introductory chapter entitled "Language and the Communication of Social Identity," Gumperz and Cook-Gumperz (1982) declare that "Social identity and ethnicity are in large part

established and maintained through language" (p. 7). Interest groups generate many new forms of language, including nonverbal forms, often of great subtlety, without any awareness that the change is taking place. Classic learning, in other words. And the different groups invariably resist pressure for standardization. In another chapter, Maltz and Borker (1982) show how participation in different small group structures leads to different speech conventions, even where individuals are raised in similar family environments. Their examples come mainly from male-female communication—and miscommunication.

CHAPTER 3: THE IMMENSITY OF CHILDREN'S LEARNING

1. See Miller's (1977) aptly titled *Spontaneous Apprentices: Children and Language* for more on children's language learning and the problems of studying it. Carey (1978) estimates that six-year-olds have mastered an average of 14,000 words "without much help from teachers." She documents the general process of learning. Children first hypothesize the probable meaning of a new word, then they gradually refine their knowledge and use in from 4 to 10 further encounters with the word in context. Rice (1990) reports that five-year-olds picked up the meaning of five test words such as *artisan, gramophone, makeshift, malicious, nurturant* and *viola,* each of which appeared seven times in a single 12-minute viewing of a television cartoon. Three-year-olds picked up an average of 1.5 words.

The subtlety of children's word learning is discussed in Linda Smith (1995). She instances a two-year-old who is told a certain object is a tractor and is immediately able to recognize and name other tractors. How does the child know the word applies to the object and not to its color, size, noise, movement, big wheels, or anything else (an old philosophical conundrum)? The answer is that there is a bias in learning, a focusing of attention that puts constraints on hypotheses that the learner might make, ruling out many logical alternatives. Children know what word meanings are possible, not because they were born with the knowledge but because they have learned that names for common objects usually refer to objects of similar shape rather than to those of a similar size. This bias can sometimes be seen in "overgeneralizations," when a child calls all four-legged animals cats, for example. A large number of studies summarized by Bates, Bretherton, and Snyder (1988) demonstrate that children don't all learn language in a similar manner. The differences lie not in the rates at which children learn nor in dependence on comprehension but in the particular circumstances in which they find themselves. The learning is adaptive, interactive, continuous, constructive—and self-organized. It is not inborn nor it is a result of maturation. Infants are not "prewired" to learn to talk. Yet by the age of two, they have learned what they should attend to in language. In other words, they have learned *how* to learn language. Many observations of the complexity and subtlety of the ways in which individual children learn are contained in Bloom (1991). After a comprehensive introduction summarizing children's language learning between the ages of two and three, there are detailed and technical reports of many studies, showing, for example, how children focus first on nouns (naming) to get an initial mastery of language, then they focus on verbs in order to construct a grammar.

2. Edward Hall's classics *The Silent Language* (1959) and *The Hidden Dimension* (1966) explore the subtlety and pervasiveness of nonverbal signs and other conventions in cultural and personal development. Elsewhere, Hall (1986) discusses the role of education in the formation of ethnic identity, addressing himself particularly to Indian cultures in the United States. He concludes from his worldwide experience that the human species is a learning organism, and that it is patently untrue that children need motivating in order to learn. They love to learn, he says, though they may not always love school (p. 159). Hall's observations are in a book devoted to global perspectives on learning and development (Thomas and Ploman, 1986).

3. Krashen (1985, 1991, 1993) has published extensively to promote the argument that learning results from "comprehensible input" in first and other languages, spoken and written. Smith (1975) argues that comprehension and learning are inseparable.

4. The relationship of members of a linguistic minority to a dominant culture is always complex and problematic, fraught with emotion and preconceptions. Membership of some "clubs" or social groups can breed intolerance and paranoia. For a general review of these problems, focusing on Australia but examining situations involving language rights in the United States, bilingualism in Canada, and "semilingual" immigrant children in Sweden, see Kalantzis, Cope, and Slade (1989). They comment that while "there are no primordial cultural differences and no cultural gaps which ultimately and irretrievably thwart communication" (p. 17), there are worldwide problems of cultural and linguistic diversity in education and assessment as well as in society in general. Plurality is not always a diversity of equals, and difference often disempowers. The world doesn't need homogeneity, and would lose a great deal if differences among cultures and people were obliterated, but great pressure toward standardization is exerted through politics, advertising, and of course education. Another powerful collection of articles about linguistic interaction and conflict is provided by Wolfson and Manes (1985). Many specific situations in different parts of the world are examined, with examples of "linguistic genocide" where entire languages— and sometimes the people who speak them—may be wiped out.

Learning, whether viewed from the classical or the official point of view, is never neutral. We learn more than we expect to learn, and more than we know we learn, from every language interaction in which we are involved, from private conversations and public dialogues (or monologues) to reading various kinds of texts and engagement with different types of media. A specialized discipline called *discourse analysis* investigates what is going on in every kind of event involving language. Complex analyses probe beneath structure and content to the multilayered "textures" of social and cultural factors behind every language interaction, ranging from reader or listener expectations and interpretations to the assumptions and often hidden agendas of speakers, writers, and publishers. Many technical volumes and articles have been published on discourse analysis since the 1980s.

The relation between language and power is a particular focus of *critical discourse analysis,* which looks for ideological contexts surrounding all speech, reading, and writing activities. The critical view deplores many aspects of language study—as it would doubtless criticize the present book—for lack of an explicit social theory. The view asserts that there is nothing about language that is timeless or "pure." There is always an agenda. Critical discourse analysis demands from authors and researchers a "grounded" perspective with "closeness" to the reality of individual people's lives (something which in general I leave readers to do). Critical discourse analysis of children's language learning would look at imbalances in the power relations of children and teachers (as members of different clubs) and at the general dynamics of the situation and institution they are in. In a reading situation, for example, they would carefully dissect the text that is involved—interpreting its place in a general social and cultural situation. The approach has deep roots in the pioneering literacy and theoretical work of Brazilian educator Paulo Freire, who asserted that in learning to read children also learn to read the world. Until exiled from his own country by a military coup in 1964, Freire taught literacy by engaging his adult peasant students in the social and political problems of their own communities. His most influential books are *Pedagogy of the Oppressed* (1972) and *Education for Critical Consciousness* (1982).

Bloome and Talwalkar (1997) provide a helpful review article of a number of critical discourse analysis studies. They contrast "school-centered" views of literacy, which focus on its contribution to a student's progress in school and assumed "success" outside, with "community" views concerned more with tensions raised by the pursuit of success, not only in school but also in home and community. They consider problems of minority group members acquiring values and attitudes of a dominant culture and of the maintenance of language and culture of the learner's home and historical community in the face of school socializing pressures. Bloome, Puro and Theodorou (1989) investigate classrooms to reveal how students "learn to be a student" and "learn to do school." See also Willinsky (1984) on the politics of standard English in the classroom and Willinsky (1990) on the politics of teaching literacy. Other relevant volumes with self-explanatory titles are Fairclough's (1989) *Language and Power,* and Lakoff's (1990) *Talking Power: The Politics of Language in Our Lives.* See also Note 4, Chapter 4 below.

5. The original 27-words-a-day study was done in Los Angeles by a teacher named Mary Smith (no relation) and was published in 1941 (M. Smith, 1941).

6. Nagy and Herman (1987) reviewed and validated earlier results as part of their own extensive research program, and they calculated that vocabularies of third-grade students ranged from 4,000 to 24,000 words, with a median annual growth rate of 3,500 words. In further studies, Nagy, Herman, and Anderson (1985) and Herman, Anderson, Pearson, and Nagy (1987) estimated that fifth-grade students are likely to encounter more than 1 million words a year, between 15,000 and 50,000 of which would be unknown. A "typical middle-grade" student would learn between 1,500 and 8,250 of these unknown words a year, an average of 4,875, regardless of whether direct instruction in vocabulary was

provided by a teacher. White, Graves, and Slater (1990) reported that fourth-grade students who spoke "standard English" at a suburban school had an average annual increase of vocabulary of 5,200 words and knew an average of 16,000 out of 19,050 words on which they were tested. For "economically disadvantaged" students at an inner city school the average annual increase was 3,300 words, while similarly categorized students at a Hawaiian school, speaking mainly a Hawaiian Creole, achieved 3,500 words a year. Differences in all these rates were attributed to the general spoken and written language experience of the students, not to instruction, and were mainly related to infrequent words.

Estimating vocabulary size is not time consuming. Start with the biggest dictionary you can find for the language in which you are interested. You will only look at 100 words, whatever the size of dictionary. Note the total number of pages in the dictionary, divide that number by 100, disregard any remainder, and look at the first word on every page that is a multiple of the result, up to 100 times the result. If there are 730 pages in the dictionary, for example, 730 divided by 100 is 7 plus a bit left over, so you look at the first word on page 7, the first word on page 14, the first word on page 21, and so on, until you reach page 700. When you have done, you will have examined 100 words spread throughout the dictionary. Don't test yourself on exact definitions, merely ask whether the word is familiar to you. Count or tally the result. Then ascertain or estimate the number of words in the dictionary. Since you sampled 100 words, you can say the number of words that were familiar to you is the percentage of words you know in the dictionary. (Now you know why you should use the biggest dictionary you can lay hands on; 68 percent of 100,000 words is better than 95 percent of 3,000.) Warning: Don't use this technique to compare yourself with anyone else, or to compare one child with another. Different people may use different criteria for saying that a word is familiar. But you can use the technique for comparing your own vocabulary before and after studying a foreign language for six months, or for comparing a group of fourth graders with an otherwise similar group of fifth graders, thereby estimating the number of words on average they must be learning in a year.

7. In an article subtitled "On Greek Gods, Cartoon Heroes, and the Social Lives of Children," Dyson (1996) shows how children develop their beliefs about the world and their identities from stories—and from such media symbols as superheroes. Adults, she notes, are often childlike in looking for "good guys" and "bad guys" in real-life situations.

CHAPTER 4: JOINING THE LITERACY CLUB

1. The importance of what children learn from the reading to them that their parents and others engage in has been extensively studied and documented, for example, in Dombey (1988), Durkin (1984), Taylor and Strickland (1986), and Teale (1981).

2. Meek (1988) examines how authors (or as she says, "texts") teach what readers learn. Among many analyses of how students who read more learn

more about reading, and about much else, see Stanovich and West (1989), Nagy, Herman, and Anderson (1985), and Krashen (1993). Elley (1989) also shows how reading, and being read to, increase vocabulary. One of my favorite examples of how children learn unsuspectedly through reading—not always to their advantage—is provided by Eckhoff (1983). She asked herself why some primary graders could produce rich and interesting stories while others wrote only miserable three-line, three-words-on-a-line pieces of nonsense. Her finding was that the children's writing reflected perfectly the way their reading primers were written. The children had learned to write exactly like the authors of their school materials.

3. All children have literacy experience before they come to school (Anderson and Stokes, 1984), and low-income minority preschool children engage in as much "literacy activity"—though of different kinds—as do "more privileged" children. See also other chapters in a volume entitled *Awakening to Literacy* edited by Goelman, Oberg, and Smith (1984). On the other hand, many children who may be officially categorized as illiterate when they leave school can in fact read, though not in a school context (see the following note).

4. Street (1993) is a collection of critical discourse studies demonstrating that literacy not only has different uses in various cultures and societies, but it also has different meanings and consequences. In his introduction, Street argues that "literacy" is not a simple skill, and that "the dominant or standard model of literacy frequently subserves the interests of national politics" (p. 1). He says the "new literacy studies," with an ethnographic perspective, show a richness and diversity of literacy practices despite pressures for uniformity. From Australia, Luke (1995) argues that reading instruction is not about skills but is about the construction of identity and social relations, examining and promoting "critical reading." Janks (1993) does a similar thing from a South African perspective. In *Empowering Minority Students,* Cummins (1989) analyzes the gulf between general "conversational" language and the "academic" and "literacy" languages emphasized in school. Abilities in these different forms of language are not, he observes, strongly related. Children unfamiliar or uncomfortable with school discourse do not necessarily lack language ability. Hull (1985), writing from a British perspective, claims that written and spoken language in schools and examinations is frequently incomprehensible to many students (who are then accused of being unable to read). Also from a British perspective, Walkerdine (1982) argues that children's learning is socially guided, not put together through reasoning or discovery. She rejects distinctions between individuals and the societies in which they exist, and asserts that identities are constructed out of clusters of social practices.

CHAPTER 5: LEARNING THROUGH LIFE

1. A compelling description of how rich and lasting learning takes place effortlessly and without conscious attention during activities in which we are immersed is provided in Csikszentmihalyi's (1990) concept of *flow*. Learning is

effortless—provided learning is possible. But as I keep reiterating, learning requires understanding, which may be very difficult. Like breathing, learning is natural and continual provided it is not impeded. Breathing is effortless and inconspicuous unless (1) your lungs are congested or otherwise dysfunctional, (2) someone is trying to suffocate you, or you are in a situation that deprives you of the air you need to breathe, or (3) you have lost the habit of breathing. The solution in every case is not to be forced to breathe, but to restore the power of the lungs, remove constraints to breathing, and restore desire. In other words, to do everything possible to make breathing easy.

2. There are countless books and articles on memory, ranging from the highly abstract and technical to the popular how-to-improve variety, many of them eminently forgettable. The classic work on the relationship of stories to remembering, especially before writing (and now computers) are supposed to have taken the pressure off memory (which I doubt), is Yates (1966). Greene (1987) briefly discusses short- and long-term memory in a readable book on the interrelationships of thought, language, and action. Morris (1988) and Reber (1989) examine our remarkable capacity for remembering things we are interested in, generally without awareness, while Bahrick and Hall (1991) examine how memories of topics we have studied fade (or become inaccessible) with disuse. Many theoretical conflicts have arisen during more than 100 years of intensive study of the everyday phenomena of memory. See for example Baddeley (1986), a concise, technical and authoritative review; Neisser (1982), an engaging collection of reports, ranging from experimental/statistical to personal/discursive about memory and everyday life; and Davies and Logie (1993), an interesting compendium on academic inquiries into practical aspects of memory, each with a commentary. Other more technical aspects of memory are sampled in pages 256–261 of the notes to Smith (1994).

3. This is not the place to get into a discussion on the controversial and often emotional issue of teaching spelling. English orthography is complex and highly unpredictable, especially when it is taught "systematically" in terms of "rules." Spelling is far more regular from the point of view of meaning rather than from the sounds of speech. There is only one way to learn to spell, and that is to remember spellings. And there is only one way to remember spellings, and that is not by committing lists to memory but by encountering words in comprehensible reading (when one is a member of the "spelling club"). For the entire rationale, see Smith (1994, Chapter 8).

4. Delpit (1988) and Cazden (1992) both argue that black and other "nonmainstream" students require explicit instruction in order to "empower them." But being told exactly what must be learned doesn't make learning any easier for anyone and can contribute to the frustration and loss of confidence of students who experience difficulty. Problems and solutions can rarely be found by examining what is taught or even how it is taught. It is the effect on the individual learner that must be studied. If an individual learns and gains confidence, then something right is being done. If the opposite occurs, then something is wrong, whatever educational or social principles are supposed to be demonstrated.

CHAPTER 6: UNDERMINING TRADITIONAL WISDOM

1. Detailed descriptions of education in the "district schools," or one-room rural or neighborhood schools, in the United States in the eighteenth and nineteenth century may be found in Butts and Cremin (1953), Church and Sedlak (1976), Cremin (1988a, 1988b), Cuban, (1984), and Power (1970), all of which I have drawn from in my discussion. There should be no nostalgia for the traditional one-room schoolhouse. The typical daily regimen was endless recitation and memorization as teachers with little experience confronted students with little interest or understanding. By the middle of the nineteenth century, schools were the topic of a good deal of public and political debate on issues that strike a familiar contemporary note. There were bitter arguments about whether reading should be taught by a "skills" or "meaning" approach and about child-centered vs. subject-centered instruction generally. There was also considerable concern about spelling. Ability to spell was believed to reflect social status and spelling instruction was seen as a means of achieving standardized pronunciation (Church and Sedlak, 1976, p. 16).

2. A fundamental question concerned who should control education, individual parents and teachers with a variety of ideas and expectations or the state with its panoply of standardized curriculums and tests. The "reform" movement for the "common schools" of the middle of the nineteenth century favored structure and organization, advocating age grading, conformity of teaching practices, and state control. One of its leaders was the influential and energetic American school reformer Horace Mann (1796–1859), founder and secretary from 1837 to 1848 of the Massachusetts Board of Education, the first state board of education in the United States. He was a prime mover in bringing Prussian educational practices to the United States.

Great reforms were initiated in all aspects of life in Prussia by its military and landowner leaders following defeats at the hand of Napoleon in 1805 and humiliation in the subsequent peace treaty in 1807. Following extensive organizational restructuring and the introduction of rigorous training programs, the army participated in defeats of Napoleon in 1813 and 1815 and was victorious in wars against Denmark, Austria, and France in the 1860s and 1870s. Prussian territory, political power, and philosophical influence reached their peak at this time. Similarly stringent methods of organization and training were applied in agriculture, including the introduction of new techniques of animal husbandry, and of course, in education. The disciplined hierarchical organization of all aspects of Prussian society was a source of great attraction to Mann and other reformers—and of great anxiety to Mann's opponents concerned with the possibility of authoritarianism in schools.

There was another aspect of Prussian education beyond standards and centralized control which might appear anomalous today but which appealed to Mann's own progressive views. Prussian classroom methodology was significantly influenced by another great 19th century educator, the Swiss theorist and teacher Johann Heinrich Pestalozzi (1746–1827), who was a proponent of child-centered education. Pestalozzi believed in individual development and concrete experience in a familial atmosphere of love and understanding, with the total elimination of memorization, fear, ridicule, and corporal punishment. The gentler aspects of the Prussian system were anathema to many of Mann's critics, notably a group of Boston school teachers who overruled him by arguing that promotion of pleasure should never be the basis of any educational system, and that learning should be difficult in order to build character (Church and Sedlak, 1976, pp. 78–79.) Prussia—and Mann—failed to gain widespread official acceptance of their principles of child-centered education. But their views on centrally organized and rigidly standardized school systems remain dominant today.

3. In an authoritative review, Mosteller, Light, and Sachs (1996) report (with "dismay") that contrary to widespread assumptions, few studies have been done on the efficacy of skills grouping—and there is no compelling evidence that it has a major impact, positive or negative, on learning. They also note that the question of optimum class size also remains open, there is clearly no simple answer, and the need is to be flexible.

4. A massive amount of research into learning has been supported by grants from the armed services (Nobel, 1989). See also Note 3, Chapter 9.

CHAPTER 7: FABRICATING A THEORY OF LEARNING

1. The bible for the early history of experimental psychology is Boring (that's the author's name) (1957). Much of the story of Hermann Ebbinghaus is recounted there. I also consulted standard biographies. Another classic book from the same era, entitled *Theories of Learning* (Hilgard, 1956), begins with the bald assertion: "The scientific study of learning is carried on primarily by psychologists . . . Professional educators have welcomed educational psychology as a foundation science upon which to build their practices . . . Under the circumstances, it is very natural for psychologists to feel that the study of learning belongs to them" (pp. 1,2). A multitude of books on learning by experimental psychologists—and more recently by cognitive scientists—have repeated the claim or taken it for granted.

2. The idea that learning is a function of time on task has a familiar corollary: "If something isn't learned the first time, teach it again" (as opposed to the classic view that if something isn't learned the first time, something is wrong with the learning situation). Both were principles of the "mastery learning" movement which held great sway in the 1970s and 1980s, based mainly on the theorizing of Benjamin Bloom (1956) and his colleagues at the University of Chicago. In addition to spawning vast amounts of systematic instructional materials, mastery learning captured 1,500 school districts, including that of Chicago, where it was ultimately pronounced a failure (see Smith, 1986). For a readable summary and trenchant critique of mastery learning, see Shannon (1984).

3. Skinner's contribution included *The Technology of Teaching* (1968), remarkable in putting all aspects of educational practice and administration into the jargon and techniques of pigeon training. On the uselessness, indeed counterproductiveness, of reward and punishment in learning, see Kohn's *Punished by Rewards* (1993).

CHAPTER 8: THE ENTRY OF THE TESTERS

1. Francis Galton was the author of a book entitled *Hereditary Genius*. Many members of his family were rich and famous, and he associated these qualifications with high intelligence and value to society. He advocated state regulated marriage among "highly gifted" people and segregation of others to prevent them from propagating. He also proposed the state ranking of individuals by ability—a practice not unheard of today—with the right to more offspring allocated to those at the top. Galton had a passion for population statistics and comparisons of all kinds, and was constantly measuring (including the first systematic examination of a school population). He refined statistical techniques that became the basis of many educational tests, work that was continued by his successors in the Chair of Eugenics at London University—Karl Pearson, Robert A. Fisher, and Cyril Burt, all renowned and influential statisticians. Burt compared children in different types of school in different regions of England between 1909 and 1911, and he thought the evidence "conclusive" that mental capacities were inherited. He was later discredited for fraudulently inventing data in a study of twins.

The British approach to eugenics was based largely on family trees and measurement. The pioneering experimental discoveries of Austrian monk Gregor Mendel (1822–1911), who for cloistered years studied the genetic transmission of characteristics of pea plants, were more influential in the United States and generally prevailed. They could be considered the ancestors of today's genetic engineering. Eugenic societies sprang up all over the world at the beginning of the twentieth century, peaking in Britain and the United States in the 1930s. The concern was that "unfit" members of society—usually categorized by scores on intelligence tests—would contaminate the breeding stock of the nation, or of the race, and constitute an intolerable economic burden. The British were usually concerned with class; the Americans with race. Many famous scientists, clerics, authors, and politicians joined these societies and made impassioned addresses, including the young Winston Churchill. Theodore Roosevelt was an early supporter, publicly expressing his fears about "race-suicide" and the "yellow peril." All major U.S. universities offered courses on eugenics, and fairs and expositions were organized to acquaint the general public of the facts. Eugenic practices, such as restrictions on marriage, controlled immigration, and enforced sterilization, continue throughout the world today.

The first leader of the eugenics movement in the United States was biologist Charles B. Davenport, who believed that heredity determined not only physical characteristics but temperament and behavior. He was convinced that the "mixture of blood" would result in more crime. Davenport promoted the usual "positive" eugenic strategies of controlled birthrates and selective immigration policy, but also recommended the "negative eugenics" of the prevention of reproduction. He preferred segregation to sterilization, but his concern over the consequences of "lust" led him to prefer castration to vasectomy because the latter did not remove desire. As a scientist he wanted more research and more data about "feeble minded" and other "defectives" in the population.

In their discussion of education in the United States after the First World War, Church and Sedlak (1976) note that "many reform-minded Americans in the pre-Hitlerian era advocated improving the nation's racial stock by keeping the unfit from breeding future generations of equally unfit people" (p. 311). In 1914, Charles A. Ellwood, a sociologist at the University of Missouri, declared that every child in the state should be "sentenced" by a compulsory education law to complete the minimum requirement of education in the public schools. For as long as the student failed to pass final examinations, or if he was sent to an institution for the feebleminded, he would not be permitted to marry or have children (cited by Church and Sedlak, p. 312). Toward the end of their lives, Galton and Davenport joined many others, like the futuristic novelist H. G. Wells, in public contemplation of the eventual necessity of involuntary sterilization of society's "unfit." Sterilization was a major part of the Nazi eugenic program in Germany in the 1930s, with operations on 225,000 "unfit" and "feebleminded" individuals in three years (Kevles, 1985, p. 117). This was independent of the state's anti-Semitic policies.

The first state sterilization law in the United States was passed in Indiana in 1907 (Kevles, 1985). By 1917, 16 states had sterilization laws, which were still on the books of 22 states in 1985. Sterilization was regarded as a humane treatment beneficial to the recipients. Those eligible for the privilege included sexual offenders, habitual criminals, epileptics, the insane, and drug addicts. Many of those sterilized on the basis of "sexual delinquency" were women. Similar laws were enacted in many parts of Europe. The depression of the 1920s and 1930s boosted the sterilization rate on both sides of the Atlantic. The view of a British biologist that parents who resorted to public assistance for child support should be "punished" with sterilization was published in the scientific journal *Nature*.

In a book produced in 1935 on behalf of the American Eugenics Society, Ellsworth Huntington earnestly outlined aspects of eugenics—"sometimes called race hygiene"—in the form of a catechism. The main object of negative eugenics, he said, was "to eliminate undesirable types of people," namely "emotional and mental defectives who are a menace or undue burden to society," and "borderline persons of low intelligence and unstable temperament who are of little direct value to society, and . . . likely to have a high percentage of defective children" (p. 39). He reflected upon the relative advantages of birth control and segregation, but he noted that sterilization was the least expensive solution.

The British had reservations about involuntary sterilization. National politicians were reluctant to vote for it and doctors questioned the legality of it. But there was a strong movement to persuade the public of its virtues. In a popular small handbook, scientist Cora Dodson (1934) lyrically describes the manner in which the "successful experiment" was conducted in California—"one of the great centers of scientific activity, not only of the United States, but of the world." In terms reminiscent of a tourist brochure she describes how psychologists advised and trained teachers on sending difficult children and the feeble-minded to special homes for preparation for the operation. Whittier School in Stockton overcame the difficulty of explaining the advantages of sterilization to "higher grade" feeble-minded in the following way: "They are made to realize, however poor and feeble, they have a part to play for the good of mankind by voluntarily allying themselves with the endeavor to prevent inherited misery in the future" (p. 20). Dodson stayed at Sonoma Home, the State Institute for the "feeble minded," where "little groups of boys and girls move to and fro . . . joking and playing as readily with the staff as with each other"—and look forward to their operation, which they regard as a reward for good work. Dodson discusses how child guidance work developed in the United States "as a result of careful study and treatment given in mental clinics, schools for delinquents, and institutions for the feeble minded." Neither money nor brains are spared, she reports, in rendering the individual content and happy (Dodson, pp. 17–18), that is, sterilized. She also describes attempts in Denmark, Switzerland, Germany and other countries to relate the question of sterilization "to the philanthropic thought and ideals which underlie all serious social effort."

More than 58,000 Americans were sterilized between 1927, when a supreme court ruling permitted eugenic sterilizations, and 1956 (Reilly, 1977). There were many sterilizations—especially of women—by the Indian Health Service and the Office of Economic Opportunity in the 1970s (Kevles, 1985). During the cold war, there was renewed controversy over the nature of intelligence, its heritability, and differences among races. Nobel prizewinning physicist William Shockley believed that heredity determined intelligence and donated his own sperm to a public scheme for the future breeding of good stock. In 1971 he proposed to the annual convention of the American Psychological Association that financial incentives should be provided to encourage sterilization among people of low intelligence (Kevles, p. 275).

There was a legal challenge in 1974 to the U.S. Department of Health, Education and Welfare regulations governing human sterilization. The judge noted that "over the last few years, an estimated 100,000 to 150,000 low-income persons have been sterilized annually under federally funded programs" (Macklin & Gaylin, 1981, p. 210), with many poor people being coerced under threat of withdrawal of funds. But the judge upheld the right to sterilize minors and mental incompetents without their consent if a "knowledgeable" decision was made on their behalf after elaborate hearing processes. (The judgment is one of several landmark decisions on sterilization printed in full in an appendix to Macklin and Gaylin.)

In Canada, the province of Alberta enacted a "Sexual Sterilization Act" in 1928, partly in response to fears that "feeble-minded" people were a menace to society (McDonald, 1996). The act was officially repealed in 1972, by which time at least 2,767 individuals had been sterilized, primarily on the basis of IQ tests. In 1997, Leillani Muir sued the Alberta Provincial Government for $2.5 million for wrongful sterilization and failure to provide her with adequate education. She said she was sterilized at the Provincial Training School for Mental Defectives at Red Deer at the age of 14, after being told only that she would have her appendix removed. She believed the same happened to many other girls.

Kevles sees a continuation of the eugenic purpose in contemporary research into genetic engineering and intelligence. Duster (1990) is troubled that great human concerns of our era, such as war, poverty, class, crime, and drug use are being attributed more to genetic than social causes. He believes that genetic science is providing the justification for old eugenics theories and solutions, and he wonders where new genetic technologies should "draw the line." The U.S. Supreme Court ruling still stands—states can sterilize if there is evidence of genetically inherited antisocial behavior. Books advocating eugenics programs, including sterilization, continue to be published, often in the name of science. A popular CD ROM dictionary, which must be on many computers including those in schools, currently defines eugenics as: "the science of improving the human race by a careful selection of parents in order to develop healthier and more intelligent children."

My summary of eugenics is largely based on Kevles (1985), a scholarly history with many fascinating biographies, comprehensively referenced. Macklin & Gaylin, (1981) is an edited volume based on a seminar on ethical issues on sterilization. It concludes that a moral community has the social responsibility to foster capacities for morally responsible behavior, that is, involuntary sterilization (p. 192). Boring (1957) contains interesting biographies of Galton, Pearson, and other leading characters in the development of statistical methods for assessing intelligence. Steven Jay Gould's *The Mismeasure of Man* (1981) is a general history and critique of the intelligence issue. Germaine Greer (1984) discusses the relation of eugenics to educational testing in *Sex and Destiny* and concludes that "modern society is unique in that it is profoundly hostile to children."

2. The chief U.S. tester in the First World War was Robert M. Yerkes, president of the American Psychological Association in 1916 and a follower of both Galton and Davenport. More than 1,700,000 recruits were assessed by educationally and culturally biased tests that were unfamiliar to many of them. It was concluded from the testing that the average white American draftee had a mental age of 13 (Kevles, 1985).

3. VanLeirsburg (1993).

4. For more details about how low-scoring students get less help, much more about inequities in instruction, and more also about the deplorable consequences of external control of teachers, see Shannon (1984, 1985, and anything else by this prolific and outspoken researcher).

CHAPTER 9: MORE SPOILS OF WAR

1. The sinking ship analogy is developed more fully in an article entitled *Let's Declare Education a Disaster and Get On With our Lives* reprinted in Smith (1995).

2. The "education's moon" speech by James E. Allen, Jr. was much later reprinted as an historical landmark in the journal *Language Arts* (Allen, 1983). It was not until the Soviet Union launched the first earth satellite, *Sputnik,* in 1957 that the U.S. federal government began to involve itself in educational policy, previously the exclusive preserve of the states. Graham (1984) painstakingly recounts gargantuan efforts by Presidents Kennedy and Johnson to boot-

strap the educational system, held responsible for "falling behind" the Russians. He concludes that federal control, even with vast sums of money, was always problematic, rarely predictable, and inevitably political, with frequent frustrations and failures. Graham cites a U.S. Office of Education task force recommendation in 1966 calling for a massive federal "moon shot" effort to avoid the "national calamity" of many children failing to learn the 3 Rs (p. 173).

3. This was at the South West Regional Laboratory for Educational Research and Development (SWRL, pronounced swirl) in Inglewood, California, one of 20 federally funded centers designed to translate the latest technological research into educational practice. It still thrives. Academic psychologists of a behavioristic bent, linguists, systems analysts, instructional designers, and media experts directed small groups of teachers in the preparation of classroom materials. For examples of the philosophy and practice that ruled at the time, see Bloom (1976), Gagne (1970), Gagne and Briggs (1974), or Popham and Baker (1970)—a few small waves in an ocean of publications on systematic objectives-based instructional design.

The dominant management methodology was sometimes familiarly known as PERT, standing for "program evaluation and review technique." A monograph issued by the U.S. Office of Education (Cook, 1966) describes concisely how PERT should be applied in education and gives a summary of its history. For example: "It was during the years of conflict that initiation of such broad, large-scale research projects as the Manhattan project [development of the atomic bomb] . . . began to reach fruition . . . In the specific case of new military weapons system [sic], because of increasing difficulty in properly managing all activities associated with its development using traditional techniques, a search began for new methods of handling a multitude of unknown and complex tasks" (pp. 1,2). This methodology became mandatory for all major research efforts coming out of the Department of Defense or the Office of Education. Teaching, if I may underline the point, was included under the heading of "a multitude of unknown and complex tasks."

The first attempt at the U.S. federal level to mandate what and how teachers should teach was the passage of Bill HR2614 through the House of Representatives in November 1997, establishing the controversial phonics approach to reading instruction as "the national reading program." Both advocates and critics of the bill saw it as a first step toward federal control of state and local curriculum, certification, staff development, and teacher education in literacy, mathematics, bilingual education, and other subject areas.

CHAPTER 10: THE OFFICIAL THEORY GOES ON-LINE

1. Cognitive scientists haven't been slow to urge the assimilation of their world view into education. A characteristic example is a book by Schank (1982) entitled *Reading and Understanding: Teaching from the Perspective of Artificial Intelligence.* The purpose of reading, he says, is to remember the information in the text, which may surprise many people who like to pass their time with books

and magazines. For an alternative view, see the chapter *What Happens When You Read* in Smith (1995). Bransford and Stein (1984) offer a guide to improving learning, thinking, and creativity based on insights from artificial intelligence. Most volumes and articles on *cognitive science* (there is a journal with that name) are technical and dense. A readable exception is *Artificial Intelligence in Psychology,* by Boden (1992). The title is not ironic.

The official theory sees learning and thinking as isolated activities taking place wholly within an individual's brain (or within the individual). The classic view that learning is inseparably interlocked with the environment—with surrounding people, objects, circumstances as well as purposes and support for accomplishing ends—has recently been revived (as something "new") in exotic areas of artificial intelligence and robotics. The contemporary idea is that the human brain is part of a "coupled system" that also includes the environment. Clark (1997), Bechtel (1997) and Varela, Thompson and Rosch (1991), have with others begun to use the term "the embodied mind" for this state of affairs. The embodiment referred to is not simply that the brain is part of the body—a significant fact often overlooked by the official theory of learning—but that the brain and the body are embodied in an environment that promotes and sustains learning. Clark also talks of "embodied cognition" in demonstrating how infant learning of such basic functions as walking is the result of an interplay of brain, body, and local environment, not a centrally coordinated function of a "blueprint in the brain." Centralization, says Clark in a remark related to learning which could be taken as a general statement, is too rigid. Circumstances always need to be "equal partners" in learning and behaving situations.

From a different theoretical point of view, derived largely from the interactionist theories of Piaget and Vygotsky, "constructivist" researchers in education stress the importance of environment and "context" in classroom situations, emphasizing "learning" over "teaching." See Fosnot (1996) and Duckworth (1987). The classic view recognizes that classrooms are diverse. The official view disregards anything occurring outside the learner's own head (apart from instruction) as irrelevant.

2. Computer terminology distinguishes *hardware,* the solid structural parts of electronic equipment, from *software,* the routines and procedures that are run by the equipment's programs. Cognitive scientists have added the concept of *wetware,* a characteristically unsubtle way of referring to the human brain and its neural networks. Connectionism, also known as "neuroscience" and "neural network theory," is a theory about wetware. It uses computer simulations to see if mindless reactive devices (like the rubber sheet described in the chapter) could replicate human learning, when the probability of "correct responses" is mathematically increased as a result of experience, and the probability of "incorrect responses" is diminished. There are examples of the procedure in Linda Smith (1995, p.10), for children's word learning, and in Nelson (1995), for aspects of German grammar. Educational psychologist Carl Bereiter (1991) provides a clear and enthusiastic account of connectionism, and Nobel prizewinning physiologist Francis Crick (1989), in an equally clear and businesslike manner, claims that connectionism is unreliable and unlike the brain in many significant respects.

3. Skinner (1985).
4. See Note 3, Chapter 5.

CHAPTER 11: LIBERATING OUR OWN LEARNING

1. Vygotsky (1978) argues that learning, and every other aspect of memory, attention, perception, and thought first develops socially and is then internalized. For discussions of the influence of Vygotsky's views in education, see Moll (1990).
2. For more on the FUN!!! approach to systematic instruction, see Smith (1986).
3. Once again, this unconscious stream of learning during absorbing activity is well described by Csikszentmihalyi's (1990) concept of *flow*.
4. The role of imagination in learning—and making sure it doesn't get lost beneath all the technology of education—is the concern of Egan and Nadaner (1988). They bring together an engaging international group of writers, scientists, philosophers, at least one musician, and a British poet laureate to share visions of creative education.
5. Meek (1996) carefully examines overt and hidden differences in books that children read, or are expected to read, during their school days. She finds a wide range of diversity and difficulties between "narrative" (or "fiction") and "information" books, all of which have a bearing on how children grow up and develop their perceptions of themselves and the world.

CHAPTER 12: LIBERATING SCHOOLS AND EDUCATION

1. For discussions and examples of teachers working together to examine and improve their own conditions, see *The Empowerment of Teachers* (Maeroff, 1988), also Newman (1991). Apple and Beane (1995) is a collection of reports on innovative "democratic schools."
2. A cautionary note: Despite the constant preoccupation with improvement and reform, schools have hardly changed during the last 100 years, according to an end-of-the-century appraisal by Jesse Goodman (1997). Education in the United States is undergoing major reconstruction for the information age, but the effect is to reinforce practices that have dominated schools throughout the twentieth century. Goodman presents his analysis in terms of Toffler's (1980) conception of technological "waves" that sweep over civilizations. According to Toffler, the first wave, the "agricultural revolution," was dominant from "sometime around" 8000 BC to the eighteenth century, when it began to be challenged by the second wave of the industrial revolution. The second wave, Toffler says, created a mass education system built on a "factory model," with an "overt curriculum" of basic reading, writing, and arithmetic, and a "covert curriculum" of punctuality, obedience, and repetitive work (p. 45). Industrialism is now being

overwhelmed by a third wave in a new "age of synthesis," with new resources, new technologies, new values, and new social structures. Toffler is optimistic about how schools will change. Goodman doesn't agree.

Goodman characterizes the core principles of second wave schools as social functionalism, efficiency and productivity, individualism, and the supremacy of experts from outside the classroom. Social functionalism, according to Goodman, is concerned with following orders and conformity. Efficiency and productivity are preoccupied with such matters as objectives, tests, and accountability. Individualism focuses on personal effort, achievement, failure, and competition. And experts are not created but followed. Schools are controlled and directed by experts rather than by teachers, parents, or students. All these, of course, are characteristic attributes of the official theory of learning that I have discussed in this book. And Goodman doesn't see any great changes in the "information age." The alternatives that he would like to see, on the other hand, all reflect the classical point of view. They include social democracy rather than "top-down" structures in schools, an emphasis on "existential experience" rather than on efficiency and productivity, collaboration rather than individualism, and teacher-driven reform in place of "experts". He observes that many individual instances can be found of teachers and principals employing these alternative approaches, usually in relative isolation and without much official support.

3. I considered one final question that I am often asked: *What is your theory called?* By asking for a name, I suspect, people want to put everything into a category. But I don't regard the arguments of this book as "theoretical"—and I have never liked theories. They sound too big, too all-embracing and impersonal, too pretentious. I prefer ideas—my own and other people's. Ideas seem to me just the right size for contemplation, confrontation, and debate. They are bigger than data (which remind me of small heaps of sand) and smaller than theories (which are like mountain ranges). One way I have tried to differentiate the "classical" and "official" approaches to learning is by calling the former a "view" and the latter a "theory." There *is* a theory at the heart of the official position, namely psychology's experimental theory of learning. The classic view may be just as widely known, if only implicitly, but it lacks official status. Experimental psychology tends simply to dismiss learning that takes place beyond the "dependent variables" that are the focus of specific experimental tasks. Learning of the kind that Eckhoff (1983) observed (Note 2, Chapter 4 above) is relegated to minor categories of "incidental learning," or "latent learning," and ignored. "Vicarious learning" is what caged rats and cats do, very minimally, when they watch other rats and cats working for rewards.

And then, as I was completing the final draft of this manuscript, an onslaught against "grand theories," especially in education, appeared in the *Harvard Educational Review*. British academic and teacher Gary Thomas (1997) says theories may be appealing, but they are often unsound and misleading. They don't warrant the status they get. He asserts that theories—he cites those of Piaget and Chomsky as examples—become dogma, despite their unreliable foundations and huge superstructures. They homogenize thought and block progress. Good ideas don't come from theory, but despite it. Thomas says that "Education is preoccupied with the paraphernalia of theory and its development," (p. 85). He points out that the prominent American philosopher and educator John Dewey was strongly opposed to theories in education, preferring "specific inquiries." He also cites approvingly French philosopher Michel Foucault's predilection for intellectual anarchy. Thomas himself favors what he calls "ad hocery"—trying to understand specific situations on specific occasions, in terms of the particular circumstances in which matters of interest arise. Discourse analysts would term this a "grounded" perspective. I see it as the classic, not the official, point of view.

ACKNOWLEDGMENTS

I am indebted, as always, to Mary-Theresa Smith for wise and patient counsel and indefatigable editing. My particular thanks, after many years and a number of books, to Carole Saltz, Peter Sieger, and Mel Berk (now retired) of Teachers College Press, who never fail to leaven competence with amicability. The book also benefited from tough encouragement by two anonymous reviewers. None of it would have been possible without the openness and interest of thousands of dedicated teachers whom I have met and learned from during my professional career in education.

References

Allen, James E., Jr. (1983). The Right to Read—Target for the 70s. *Language Arts, 60,* 1, 100–101.

Anderson, Alonzo B., and Shelley J. Stokes. (1984). Social and Institutional Influences on the Development and Practice of Literacy. In Hillel Goelman, Antoinette Oberg, and Frank Smith (Eds.), *Awakening to Literacy.* Exeter, NH: Heinemann.

Apple, Michael W., and James A. Beane. (1995). *Democratic Schools.* Alexandria, VA: Association for Supervision and Curriculum Development.

Bahrick, Harry P., and Lynda K. Hall. (1991). Lifetime Maintenance of High School Mathematics Content. *Journal of Experimental Psychology: General, 120,* 1, 20–33.

Bates, Elizabeth, Inge Bretherton, and Lynn Snyder. (1988). *From First Words to Grammar.* Cambridge, UK: Cambridge University Press.

Bereiter, Carl. (1991). Implications of Connectionism for Thinking about Rules. *Educational Researcher, 20,* 3, 10–16.

Bloom, Benjamin S. (1976). *Human Characteristics and School Learning.* New York: McGraw Hill.

Bloom, Benjamin S., et al. (1956). *Taxonomy of Educational Objectives. Handbook I: Cognitive Domain.* New York: McKay.

Bloom, Lois. (1991). *Language Development from Two to Three.* Cambridge, UK: Cambridge University Press.

Bloome, David, Pamela Puro, and Erine Theodorou. (1989). Procedural Display and Classroom Lessons. *Curriculum Inquiry, 19,* 3, 265–291.

Bloome, David, and Susan Talwalkar. (1997). Book Reviews: Critical Discourse Analysis and the Study of Reading and Writing. *Reading Research Quarterly, 32,* 1, 104–112.

Boden, Margaret A. (1989). *Artificial Intelligence in Psychology.* Cambridge, MA: MIT Press.

Boring, Edwin G. (1957). *A History of Experimental Psychology*. New York: Appleton-Century-Crofts.

Bransford, John D., and Barry S. Stein. (1984). *The IDEAL Problem Solver: A Guide for Improving Thinking, Learning and Creativity*. New York: Freeman.

Butts, R. Freeman, and Lawrence A. Cremin. (1953). *A History of Education in American Culture*. New York: Holt.

Carey, Susan. (1978). The Child as Word Learner. In Morris Halle, J. Breslin, and George A. Miller (Eds.), *Linguistic Theory and Psychological Reality*. Cambridge, MA: MIT Press.

Cazden, Courtney B. (1992). *Whole Language Plus: Essays on Literacy in the United States and New Zealand*. New York: Teachers College Press.

Church, Robert L., and Michael W. Sedlak. (1976). *Education in the United States: An Interpretive History*. New York: Free Press.

Cook, Desmond L. (1966). *Program Evaluation and Review Technique: Applications in Education*. Washington, DC: U.S. Department of Health, Education and Welfare.

Cremin, Lawrence A. (1988a). *American Education: The National Experience (1783–1876)*. New York: Harper.

Cremin, Lawrence A. (1988b). *American Education: The Metropolitan Experience (1876–1980)*. New York: Harper.

Crick, Francis. (1989). The Recent Excitement About Neural Networks. *Nature, 337,* 129–132.

Csikszentmihalyi, Mihaly. (1990). *Flow—The Psychology of Optimal Experience*. New York: Harper & Row.

Cuban, Larry. (1984). *How Teachers Taught: Constancy and Change in American Classrooms, 1890–1980*. New York: Academic Press.

Cummins, Jim. (1989). *Empowering Minority Students*. Sacramento, CA: California Association for Bilingual Education.

Davies, Graham M., and Robert H. Logie (Eds.). (1993). *Memory in Everyday Life*. Amsterdam: North-Holland.

Delpit, Lisa D. (1988). The Silenced Dialogue: Power and Pedagogy in Educating Other People's Children. *Harvard Educational Review, 58,* 280–298.

Dodson, Cora B. S. (1934). *Human Sterilization Today: A Survey of the Present Position*. London: Watts.

Dombey, Henriette. (1988). Stories at Home and at School. In Martin Lightfoot and Nancy Martin (Eds.), *The Word for Teaching Is Learning: Essays for James Britton*. London: Heinemann.

Duckworth, Eleanor. (1987). *"The Having of Wonderful Ideas" and Other Essays on Teaching and Learning*. New York: Teachers College Press.

Durkin, Dolores. (1984). Poor Black Children Who Are Successful Readers: An Investigation. *Urban Education, 19,* 53–76.

Duster, Troy. (1990). *Backdoor to Eugenics*. New York: Routledge.

Dyson, Anne Haas. (1996). Cultural Constellations and Childhood Identities: On Greek Gods, Cartoon Heroes, and the Social Lives of Children. *Harvard Educational Review, 66,* 4, 471–495.

Eckhoff, Barbara. (1983). How Reading Affects Children's Writing. *Language Arts, 60,* 5, 607–616.

Egan, Kieran, and Dan Nadaner (Eds.). (1988). *Imagination and Education.* Milton Keynes, UK: Open University Press.

Elley, Warwick. (1989). Vocabulary Acquisition from Listening to Stories. *Reading Research Quarterly, 24,* 2, 174–187.

Fairclough, Norman. (1989). *Language and Power.* London: Longman.

Fosnot, Catherine T. (Ed.). (1996). *Constructivism: Theory, Perspectives, and Practice.* New York: Teachers College Press.

Freire, Paulo. (1972). *Pedagogy of the Oppressed.* New York: Herder and Herder.

Freire, Paulo. (1982). *Education for Critical Consciousness.* New York: Continuum.

Gagne, Robert M. (1970). *The Conditions of Learning* (2nd ed.). New York: Holt, Rinehart and Winston.

Gagne, Robert M., and Leslie J. Briggs. (1974). *Principles of Instructional Design.* New York: Holt, Rinehart and Winston.

Goelman, Hillel, Antoinette Oberg, and Frank Smith (Eds.). (1984). *Awakening to Literacy.* Exeter, NH: Heinemann.

Goodman, Jesse. (1997). Change Without Difference: School Restructuring in Historical Perspective. *Harvard Educational Review, 67,* 1, 1–29.

Gould, Steven Jay. (1981). *The Mismeasure of Man.* New York: Norton.

Graham, Hugh Davis. (1984). *The Uncertain Triumph: Federal Education Policy in the Kennedy and Johnson Years.* Chapel Hill, NC: University of North Carolina Press.

Greene, Judith. (1987). *Memory, Thinking and Language: Topics in Cognitive Psychology.* London: Methuen.

Greer, Germaine. (1984). *Sex and Destiny: The Politics of Human Fertility.* New York: Harper & Row.

Gumperz, John J. (Ed.). (1982). *Language and Social Identity.* Cambridge, UK: Cambridge University Press.

Gumperz, John J., and Jenny Cook-Gumperz. (1982). Introduction: Language and the Communication of Social Identity. In John J. Gumperz (Ed.), *Language and Social Identity.* Cambridge, UK: Cambridge University Press.

Hall, Edward T. (1959). *The Silent Language.* New York: Doubleday.

Hall, Edward T. (1966). *The Hidden Dimension.* New York: Doubleday.

Hall, Edward T. (1986). Unstated Features of the Cultural Context of Learning. In Alan Thomas and Edward W. Ploman (Eds.). (1986). *Learning and Development: A Global Perspective.* Toronto, ON: Ontario Institute for Studies in Education.

Herman, Patricia A., Richard C. Anderson, P. David Pearson, and William E. Nagy. (1987). Incidental Acquisition of Word Meaning from Expositions with Varied Text Features. *Reading Research Quarterly, 22,* 3, 263–284.

Hilgard, Ernest. (1956). *Conditions of Learning* (2nd ed.). Englewood Cliffs, NJ: Appleton-Century-Crofts.

Hull, Robert. (1985). *The Language Gap: How Classroom Dialogue Fails.* London: Methuen.

Huntington, Ellsworth. (1935). *Tomorrow's Children: The Goal of Eugenics*. New York: Wiley.

Janks, Hilary. (1993). *Language, Identity and Power*. Johannesburg: Hodder and Stoughton.

Kalantzis, Mary, Bill Cope, and Diana Slade. (1989). *Minority Languages and Dominant Culture: Issues of Education, Assessment and Social Equity*. London: Falmer.

Kevles, Daniel J. (1985). *In the Name of Eugenics: Genetics and the Uses of Human Heredity*. New York: Knopf.

Kohn, Alfie. (1993). *Punished by Rewards*. New York: Houghton Mifflin.

Krashen, Stephen D. (1985). *The Input Hypothesis: Issues and Implications*. New York: Longman.

Krashen, Stephen D. (1991). *Fundamentals of Language Education*. Torrance, CA: Laredo.

Krashen, Stephen D. (1993). *The Power of Reading: Insights from the Research*. Englewood, CO: Libraries Unlimited.

Lakoff, Robin. (1990). *Talking Power: The Politics of Language in Our Lives*. New York: Basic Books.

Luke, Allan. (1995). When Basic Skills and Information Processing Just Aren't Enough: Rethinking Reading in New Times. *Teachers College Record, 97*, 1, 95–115.

Macklin, Ruth, and Willard Gaylin (Eds.). (1981). *Mental Retardation and Sterilization: A Problem of Competency and Paternalism*. New York: Plenum.

Maeroff, Gene I. (1988). *The Empowerment of Teachers*. New York: Teachers College Press.

Maltz, Daniel D., and Ruth A. Borker. (1982). A Cultural Approach to Male-Female Miscommunication. In John J. Gumperz (Ed.), *Language and Social Identity*. Cambridge, UK: Cambridge University Press.

McDonald, Ruth Marina. (1996). *A Policy of Privilege: The Alberta Sexual Sterilization Program, 1928–1972*. Thesis submitted in partial fulfillment of requirements for MA degree, Department of History, University of Victoria.

Mead, Margaret. (1976). *Growing Up in New Guinea*. New York: Morrow.

Meek, Margaret. (1988). How Texts Teach What Readers Learn. In Martin Lightfoot and Nancy Martin (Eds.), *The Word for Teaching Is Learning: Essays for James Britton*. London: Heinemann.

Meek, Margaret. (1996). *Information and Book Learning*. Stroud, UK: Thimble.

Miller, George A. (1977). *Spontaneous Apprentices: Children and Language*. New York: Seabury.

Moll, Luis C. (Ed.). (1990). *Vygotsky and Education: Instructional Implications and Applications of Sociohistorical Psychology*. Cambridge, UK: Cambridge University Press.

Morris, P. E. (1988). Expertise and Everyday Memory. In M. M. Gruneberg, P. E. Morris, and R. N. Sykes (Eds.), *Practical Aspects of Memory: Current Research and Issues, Vol I: Memory in Everyday Life*. Chichester, UK: Wiley.

Mosteller, Frederick, Richard J. Light, and Jason A. Sachs. (1996). Sustained Inquiry in Education: Lessons from Skill Grouping and Class Size. *Harvard Educational Review, 66*, 4, 797–842.

Nagy, William E., Patricia A. Herman, and Richard C. Anderson. (1985). Learning Words from Context. *Reading Research Quarterly, 20,* 2, 233–253.

Neisser, Ulric (Ed.). (1982). *Memory Observed: Remembering in Natural Contexts.* San Francisco: Freeman.

Nelson, Charles A. (Ed.). (1995). *Basic and Applied Perspectives on Learning, Cognition, and Development.* Mahwah, NJ: Erlbaum.

Newman, Judith M. (1991). *Interwoven Conversations: Learning and Teaching Through Critical Reflection.* Toronto: Ontario Institute for Studies in Education.

Noble, Douglas D. (1989). Mental Material: The Militarization of Learning and Intelligence in U.S. Education. In Les Levidow and Kevin Robins (Eds.), *Cyborg Worlds: The Making of the Military Information Society.* London: Free Association Press.

Popham, W. James, and Eva L. Baker. (1970). *Systematic Instruction.* Englewood Cliffs, NJ: Prentice-Hall.

Power, Edward J. (1970). *Main Currents in the History of Education.* New York: McGraw Hill.

Reber, Arthur S. (1989). Implicit Learning and Tacit Knowledge. *Journal of Experimental Psychology: General, 118,* 219–235.

Reilly, Philip. (1977). *Genetics, Law, and the Social Policy.* Cambridge, MA: Harvard University Press.

Rice, Mabel L. (1990). Preschoolers' QUIL: Quick Incidental Learning of Words. In Gina Conti-Ramsden and Catherine E. Snow (Eds.), *Children's Language* (Volume 7). Hillsdale, NJ: Erlbaum.

Schank, Roger B. (1982). *Reading and Understanding: Teaching from the Perspective of Artificial Intelligence.* Hillsdale, NJ: Lawrence Erlbaum Associates.

Shannon, Patrick. (1984). Mastery Learning in Reading and the Control of Teachers and Students. *Language Arts, 61,* 5, 484–493.

Shannon, Patrick. (1985). Reading Instruction and Social Class. *Language Arts, 62,* 6, 604–613.

Skinner, B. F. (1968). *The Technology of Teaching.* New York: Meredith.

Skinner, B. F. (1985). Cognitive Science and Behaviorism. *British Journal of Psychology, 76,* 3, 291–301.

Smith, Frank. (1975). *Comprehension and Learning.* New York: Holt, Rinehart and Winston.

Smith, Frank. (1986). *Insult to Intelligence: The Bureaucratic Invasion of Our Classrooms.* Portsmouth, NH: Heinemann.

Smith, Frank. (1994). *Understanding Reading* (5th ed.). Mahwah, NJ: Erlbaum.

Smith, Frank. (1995). *Between Hope and Havoc.* Portsmouth, NH: Heinemann.

Smith, Linda. (1995). Self-Organizing Processes in Learning to Learn Words: Development Is Not Induction. In Charles A. Nelson (Ed.), *Basic and Applied Perspectives on Learning, Cognition, and Development.* Mahwah, NJ: Erlbaum.

Smith, Mary K. (1941). Measurement of the Size of General English Vocabulary through the Elementary Grades and High School. *Genetic Psychology Monographs, 24,* 311–345.

Stanovich, Keith, and Richard F. West. (1989). Exposure to Print and Orthographic Processing. *Reading Research Quarterly, 24,* 4, 402–433.

Street, Brian (Ed.). (1993). *Cross-Cultural Approaches to Literacy*. Cambridge, UK: Cambridge University Press.

Street, Brian. (1984). *Literacy in Theory and Practice*. Cambridge, UK: Cambridge University Press.

Taylor, Denny, and Dorothy S. Strickland. (1986). *Family Storybook Reading*. Portsmouth, NH: Heinemann.

Teale, William H. (1981). Parents Reading to Their Children: What We Know and Need to Know. *Language Arts, 58,* 8, 902–912.

Thomas, Alan, and Edward W. Ploman (Eds.). (1986). *Learning and Development: A Global Perspective*. Toronto, ON: Ontario Institute for Studies in Education.

Thomas, Gary. (1997). What's the Use of Theory? *Harvard Educational Review, 67,* 1, 75–104.

Toffler, Alvin. (1980). *The Third Wave*. New York: Morrow.

VanLeirsburg, Peggy. (1993). Standardized Reading Tests: Then and Now. In Jerry L. Johns (Ed.), *Literacy: Celebration and Challenge*. Bloomington, IL: Illinois Reading Council.

Vygotsky, Lev S. (1978). *Mind in Society: The Development of Higher Psychological Processes*. Cambridge, MA: Harvard University Press.

Walkerdine, Valerie. (1982). From Context to Text: A Psychosemantic Approach to Abstract Thought. In M. Beveridge (Ed.), *Children Thinking Through Language*. London: Arnold.

White, Thomas G., Michael F. Graves, and Wayne H. Slater. (1990). Growth of Reading Vocabulary in Diverse Elementary Schools: Decoding and Word Meaning. *Journal of Educational Psychology, 82,* 2, 281–290.

Willinsky, John. (1984). *The Well-Tempered Tongue: The Politics of Standard English in the Classroom*. New York: Lang.

Willinsky, John. (1990). *The New Literacy: Redefining Reading and Writing in the Schools*. London: Routledge.

Wolfson, Nessa, and Joan Manes (Eds.). (1985). *Language of Inequality*. Berlin: Mouton.

Yates, Frances A. (1966). *The Art of Memory*. London: Routledge and Kegan Paul.

Name Index

Subject Index

About the Author

Frank Smith was a reporter, editor, and novelist before beginning his formal research into language, thinking, and learning. He gained his Ph.D. at the Center for Cognitive Studies at Harvard University and has been a professor at the Ontario Institute for Studies in Education, the University of Toronto, the University of Victoria, British Columbia, and the University of the Witwatersrand, South Africa. He lives on Vancouver Island, Canada. Frank Smith has published twenty-one books and many articles on topics central to education. He has spoken at educational conferences and worked with teachers and students in Africa, North and South America, South East Asia, Australasia, and Europe.